RAISING RABBITS

not elephants

RAISING RABBITS

not elephants

an exploration of
the GSE process
of church planting

TONY WEBB

BMH Custom Book
bmhbooks.com
P.O. Box 544
Winona Lake, IN 46590

Raising Rabbits, Not Elephants
An Exploration of the GSE Process of Church Planting

© 2013 by Tony Webb

ISBN: 978-0-88469-285-0
RELIGION/ Christian Church/ Growth

Published by BMH Books, Box 544, Winona Lake, Ind. 46590 USA
bmhbooks.com

Scripture quotations marked NIV are taken from the Holy Bible, New International Version© NIV©. Copyright © 1973, 1978, 1984, by Biblica, Inc.™ Used by permission of Zondervan. All rights reserved worldwide. (www.zondervan.com)
Scripture quotations marked NASB are taken from the New American Standard Bible, © Copyright 1960, 1995 by the Lockman Foundation. Used by permission. (www.lockman.org)
Scripture quotations marked NLT are taken from the Holy Bible, New Living Translation, Copyright © 1996, 2004. Used by permission of Tyndale House Publishers, Inc., Wheaton, Illinois 60189. All rights reserved.
Scripture quotations marked MSG are taken from *The Message*. Copyright © 1993, 1994, 1995, 1996, 2000, 2001, 2002. Used by permission of NavPress Publishing Group.
The author has added italics to Scripture and quotations for emphasis.

CONTENTS

ACKNOWLEDGMENTS

There are so many who are key to seeing this project come from a growth concept birthed in the early 1990s to today.

Jesus – You are a genius and truly amazing! The way You lead us and how You have us in the harvest are all amazing – all praise to You! Thanks!

To my greatest gift from God (after my personal salvation) – my wife, Cathy. You are amazing and I am so blessed to go through this life's journey with you. Your tireless love and encouragement to keep me (us) going with these ideas, your personal passion for and in the harvest always inspire me. Thanks for everything!

My sincere thanks go to my VisionOhio (VO) covenant group. In VO, we have chosen to relate to each other through relational covenant first, which is foremost the commitment to give, and ministry/church planting second. A powerful team of men who have helped me hone ideas and concepts over the years to help form us where we are today. Nathan Wells, Andy Shank, Ron Boehm and Martin Guerena – thanks men, the journey in love focused in the harvest is great. Thanks to Terry Hofecker who was part of our covenant group for many years until God did something different – Terry, your insights and love to these ideas and me are powerful.

I am thankful for Doug Shotsky, the first gatherer. Doug and I enjoyed many years on a journey trying to figure things out. Doug, the conversation and prayer sessions were powerful and shaping – thanks for your willingness to go new places! I love all the time together, all the time.

I also thank Mac Cordell, the first E (elder) in the first GSE. Mac, Melissa, Cathy and I had many conversations and prayer sessions to seek Jesus on what He was up to. I also thank Mac because, as a reporter, he has a keen eye for words and writing; making sense. Mac tirelessly worked through the manuscript early on to help me stay on track in the writing process. Thanks to Steve Shiplett for his great capturing in colorful chart form of what was circling in my mind. You asked the right questions to make it all work.

My thanks also go to two churches that are continuing to field test GSE concepts. White Stone is a new church that has Josh Brader working tirelessly as a powerful gatherer. White Stone is also a great church family to continue to work what Jesus desires and see Him do incredible things. Jacksontown is another new church that has two gatherers working very hard, working solely in the harvest, to see the gospel spread. Chery Garvin and Carey Mariele are doing a splendid job and inspiring us all.

Thanks are also due to Terry White and the team at BMH. Thanks, Terry, for your hard work at making this entire book move ahead and taking a risk such as this.

Acts 16:5 – a church a day! Please Lord Jesus, bring a new church a day to our region!

FOREWORD

When Tony Webb first approached me about his writing a book that related to planting churches in the "flyover territories" of North America I was intrigued. Years ago, on the heels of my own dissertation work, I had written a book about starting churches in small towns. I knew by experience and research that small towns, with populations of fewer than 10,000 residents, were golden opportunities for starting churches and building regional momentum. One chapter was called, "What Wal-Mart Knows About Church Planting," reminding readers that new churches could thrive in places other than suburban North America.

Tony was looking to do the same thing, only with the next largest census demographic—"micropolitan" communities. These mid-sized, self-contained places of up to 50,000 residents were part of Tony's own experience and passion. Nice places, many in need of a fresh expression of the gospel, and they were everywhere. How could those concerned about spreading the gospel in micropolitan places be encouraged with a proven and affordable strategy to plant new churches? Tony had some ideas—good ones. After spending time with him, learning his story, and understanding his reproducible GSE ("Gatherer-Shepherd-Elder") model, I knew he was on to something that could help a lot of us. I think I said, "Hey, if you ever do write this book, please let me write the Foreword!"

New paradigms are often stumbled upon, not architected, and such is the case with the GSE process. As a church planter with his wife, Cathy, Tony intuited that some types of church planting are simply too cumbersome and too expensive to allow for the grand scale reproduction that is necessary to evangelize our continent. Besides, many gifted evangelists and gatherers we unnecessarily sidelined from functioning in their true calling because the categories didn't exist for them to be deployed. GSE opens the doors and empowers leaders in significant ways to play critical roles in seeing new works underway. I'm grateful that Tony dignifies the role of Gatherer by offering specific job descriptions, which make missional involvement achievable. I love the stories told in this book, and I love the stories, which will be told because of this book.

Raising Rabbits is a thorough but not exhausting reminder of the landscape of North American church planting. It is thoughtfully researched, and it serves as a compendium of the statistical realities, which face all those who care about the advancement of God's Great Commission. It is theologically compelling. And it is one of the only works in current church planting literature that particularly addresses micropolitan areas. The practical steps offered here allow for reproducible and affordable church planting across the spectrum of places large and small within our regions. You will be challenged and encouraged as you read. You will be even further encouraged as you imagine doors swinging open to make it possible for a widening pool of church planting participants to engage in their true life calling.

Somehow all of this got me thinking about my small town days in northeast Wisconsin, and the best birthday present I ever received. I was turning 13, and an elderly neighbor and friend named Johnny arranged to have an asphalt basketball court built for me on our family property. It was quite a gift for an impoverished man to give, considering he lived in a tiny one-room apartment. I remember the thrilling day we met with the contractor, and how he drew out a map of the work to be done, next to an outbuilding we had. It would be thirty-three feet long and thirty feet wide. Two weeks later, when the workers came to build the court, I was understandably excited as I watched from my bedroom window. But something didn't make sense. The asphalt company was moving dirt and preparing the ground on the wrong side of the building!

I was only 13, but I eventually mustered the courage to approach the workers. I got the man's attention and yelled, "Aren't you supposed to be digging over there?" The man handed me a clipboard, with the map on it, to show me that they knew what they were doing. I looked at the map, and then at the man, and then at the outbuilding. Without saying a word, I turned the clipboard 90 degrees, showing him that his crew was totally disoriented. He uttered an expletive, and then they spent a few hours patching up the area before they restarted the project on the correct side of the building.

Of course, looking back, all of that confusion and wasted time and energy could have been avoided had the map been oriented with a simple "N", and an arrow, pointing toward true north. Maps are only good if they are properly aligned with reality.

In advancing the gospel, a lot of energy and resources are wasted in moving dirt on the wrong side of the building. *Raising Rabbits* stands out as a work that points us toward true north. Allow it to properly orient you, challenge you, and encourage you to move your mission toward effective, sustainable multiplication.

Dr. Tom Nebel
Director of Church Planting
Converge Worldwide

FOREWORD

Hi Joshua,

It has been great to spend some time with you again reviewing your vision for church planting, and your book, and I consider it an honor and a privilege to write this foreword for your book.

I have known Pastor Tony Webb for many years. As a matter of fact, it was in the mid '80s that I first met him and interviewed him. He was a student at Grace Theological Seminary. I was the Director of Church Planting for [Grace Brethren] Home Missions. He came to my office a couple of times, and I interviewed him for a potential church planting job. I realized very early on that he is a young man who has great leadership skills. It did not take me very long to be able to understand him.

In the area of *acceptance of responsibility* he was "off the charts," so to speak. He had a great work ethic, he understood the value of planning, of doing what you need to do to get the goal done. Also, there is no question that he filled the role of Matthew 5:41, where Jesus said, "If someone asks you to go a mile, you go with him two." He was a second miler . . . a two- or three- miler . . . with people. He had great vision for the future, for reaching his goals. He had a great work ethic.

In the area of *compliance to the rules*, to his credit, he was not a legalist. But I could see the fruit of the Spirit in his life, and his lifestyle, and in his way of living. In the way he approached his job and work, it was obvious he understood the rules.

I also saw the *technical competence* in his life. As it says in 2 Timothy 2:15 ("study to show thyself approved" – agonize, if you will) he was a worker. He stood and worked at what he did, and he did it very well. As a matter of fact, around his peers he was known as an authority on the Greek language. Also, he well knew the value of prayer. He was an interesting combination. He was very bright, but he was also a great prayer warrior. And my experience has told me that this is a rare combination.

I also saw his value of people. . . his *interpersonal relationships*. He has a great gift in this way. As a matter of fact, I am sure that the verse in 2 Timothy 2:2 where Paul was talking to Timothy ("The things that thou hast heard of me among many witnesses, the same commit thou to faithful men, who shall teach others also") there is no question that this was something very prime in his life. . . of teaching other men to reach others also, as well as his application of Ephesians 4:11-12. What this means is equipping the saints to do their work as gifted. He was good at this. It is not making men like a bunch of sausages! It is using the gifts that God has given them for the glory of the Lord.

He has a beautiful wife. She excels, and I would say that she is a Proverbs 31 gifted lady. She is a nurse, so there is no question that she is a gifted caregiver. But she is also very gifted as a pastor's wife. She keeps a beautiful home. She supports Pastor Tony at every turn in his life and in his ministry. She is a genuine, beautiful pastor's wife.

She is also a people person. They did well as a couple. Their union produced two children. Their daughter Heather now is married to a cadet from West Point – Matt. He is an infantry officer at Ft. Bliss, Texas. They also have a son Philip, who is very bright. He managed to make it through Grace College in three years! Then he married a CPA named Leah. He is now finishing his master's work at San Jose State University getting ready to move on to Ph.D. work.

It is such a joy for me as a pastor/teacher, and a church planter myself, to know the vision this young man has for church planting. As a matter of fact, he was sent to Gettysburg, Pennsylvania, for his first church plant – a very difficult church plant. He did very well there. He was there a number of years. And then he was called to Warsaw, Indiana, where he became an associate pastor at the Community Grace Brethren Church.

On a certain Sunday morning I was sitting in that church, where I was a member. This young pastor gave a message on the church of Laodicea. I sat there as an old elder, and I was not alone. There were number of old elders sitting there with me – well educated, old elders – professors, teachers from Grace Schools – and this young man brought a message on the church of Laodicea. He preached a powerful, powerful message. As a matter of fact, at the door I shook his hand and said, "Thank you for the message. It was a very, very applicable message for me as an old elder."

I also said, "There is a rumor that you might become a Greek professor at Grace Schools. Pastor, let me tell you, what we need is young pastors who have the courage and the wherewithal to preach the message you preached this morning! I know to preach the message you had to spent a lot of time on your knees in prayer before you did it, and then you had a lot of courage to speak the message that you spoke this morning." He said, "Thank you." And nothing more was said. I also mentioned to Pastor Tony, "Greek professors are a dime a dozen, but good pastors – they are priceless!"

Time marched on. I moved to Columbus, Ohio. I had retired from Home Missions. I got a call from Pastor Tony Webb saying, "Ed, I am looking to pastor a church somewhere else. Do you have any suggestions?" I said, "Yes, I just happen to have met with a man yesterday and there is a church in Grove City (SW Columbus, Ohio) of about 30 people . . . it has been there a long time, they are in rented facilities and they are looking for a pastor."

He came, he candidated and they called him as their pastor. In a very short period of time the congregation began to grow. And lo and behold, would you believe they bought land! They got a set of plans for their building and we employed yokefellows from Grace Brethren Men International – contracted plumbers, electricians, architects – who assisted in the building of this new building. It was a beautiful building.

The congregation grew. And then a second time the yokefellows came, and built an addition to that church. And in the meantime there was a new church started in Grove City, another on the west side of Columbus, an attempt at a Hispanic plant, another church

Raising Rabbits, Not Elephants

in Mt. Sterling and another in Plain City, Ohio, as a result of Pastor Tony's ministry.

And then, through his work ethic and his astuteness, he became "Dr. Tony Webb." There was an organization in Ohio that had been organized in the mid 1990s. Now, Dr. Tony Webb has been selected as the executive director of VisionOhio. Well, it is interesting that there are right now almost twenty new points of light or church starts in Ohio.

The West Penn District in Pennsylvania is looking at sharing in the same vision as well as Indiana and a part of Georgia, all part of Dr. Webb's vision of church planting. The vision has now reached out past the state of Ohio into other locations. It is a joy for me to say, "To God be the glory."

Because of His Grace,
Caleb (Pastor Ed Jackson)

xii

SECTION 1
GSE

Chapter 1

Simple, Age-Old, Highly-Efficient and Cost-Effective

THE GATHERER/SHEPHERD/ELDER (GSE) PROCESS OF CHURCH PLANTING

"Don't let what you cannot do interfere with what you can do."
John Wooden

"Make everything as simple as possible, but not simpler."
Albert Einstein

"Peace be to you; just as the Father has sent me, so I am sending you."
Jesus Christ

Imagine a church-planting process that is simple, age-old, highly efficient, and cost-effective. How could something like that exist? Imagine a day in which a church, an individual, or an apostle can plant many churches with this lineup.

We no longer need to imagine! You are tapped by Jesus Christ to plant a new church, empowered by Him for a work that does not have any financial cost or dedicated "mission budget" line. How does that work?

Here is a story to begin our exploration of this process.

A Gatherer

Doug greeted us as we walked in the door of Ben and Joy's restaurant. Life-changing meals are not common to me. I enjoy food quite a bit, but I was not expecting all that God had in mind with this amazing meal on this particular summer evening.

My wife, Cathy, and I were considering relocating to a small town called Mount Sterling, south of Grove City, a southwest suburb of Columbus, Ohio. We wanted to continue in our local church, which was in Grove City, but we wanted a small-town feel for the second half of our life together. So, we went to Ben and Joy's to eat. We had heard of Ben and Joy's for a while and finally decided that since the kids were gone at a youth conference, it was time to explore. We had no idea how this simple decision would result in something much bigger. Only Jesus could make it so.

We walked into the restaurant, and Doug greeted us. He said, "I do not know you. Why don't you sit over there, and I will be right with you." So we sat where Doug pointed.

As our meal began, Doug shared with us the meal options, and we ended up enjoying the delicious buffet. What was life-changing about the meal was not the food—though it was incredibly good. As we both watched Doug work the restaurant that evening, Cathy summarized it well: "I bet he would be an amazing evangelist—if he is saved."

Not knowing where Doug stood on the Jesus question, we continued with our evening. I saw that Doug seemed fascinated with everyone—especially us because he did not know us. He came by frequently to find out more about us. I think he was more interested in us than we were in him. He asked questions about us and particularly why we were there in his town. We shared a little about moving to Mount Sterling, but did not mention planting a church.

Finally he asked us: "You look too young to retire, so why are you here in Mount Sterling tonight?" I felt this was a God-given opportunity. I had one of those "two-seconds-feels like 10 years" moments, thinking, "Do I really tell him why we are here tonight or do I not?

I said, "We are here to see if God wants us to plant a new church in Mount Sterling."

Doug then exclaimed, "That is amazing! I am a believer, and I would love to see a new church here."

We left the restaurant that evening recognizing that we had met a "gatherer." I had met many people like Doug before, but never in a context such as God had prepared that night in Ben and Joy's restaurant. Cathy and I mused about all the ways we could plant a church with someone like Doug: a young man, single, a lover of Jesus Christ, a sharer of His love.

I also left the restaurant that night with Doug's phone number, and called him early the next week, hoping he remembered me. He did! He said later that he had offered his assistance on other church related projects, even other church plants, but I was the first person to call him back and take him up on the offer.

Over the next two years, Doug and I met regularly to share, dream and pray. During that time, Doug met and married Marlaina and now they have a son, William, who was recently dedicated at the new church in Mount Sterling. This new church, called Sterling Grace, is the very church Doug and Marlaina were/are instrumental in planting. That was six years ago.

What God Did

Doug and I used those first two years to get to know each other and to find out if we really wanted to plant a church together. We talked, prayed, and dreamed. We brought Marlaina on board. We decided that Doug and Marlaina would function in the gathering role, and Cathy and I would function in the shepherding role.

This Gatherer/Shepherd/Elder (GSE) process worked as Doug gathered and invited people to come to the church. I was the shepherd. We prayed that God would raise up an elder/pastor from our own small group. God said "yes" to this prayer.

Gatherer: A gatherer is a person, a man or a woman, who is a people magnet; someone who is very natural in personal makeup in connecting to other people. They are ones who are open to a new vision of how to work in the harvest together in forming new churches.

Shepherd: A person gifted from Jesus as a shepherd; someone who is willing to use their gift to see spiritual well-being develop among those gathered.

Elder: A biblically qualified elder who enters the group sometime down the road. Takes the newly formed church to greater biblical establishment.

We met for more than two years with Doug functioning as gatherer and me as shepherd. We saw a number of families visit, then move away from the area. It was frustrating. We often asked God what He was up to. Doug would connect with people and invite them to come. They would come and love what we were doing. Then they would move away, either for work or some other reason. Meanwhile we prayed for God to raise up our pastor out of the church. From among those families that Doug had gathered, a man named Mac and his wife, Melissa, emerged. They had connected to Sterling Grace, and we had had some time to get to know them. One day, early in the process, while we were meeting at Doug's house, Doug said, "I think Mac may be our next pastor."

I tried really hard not to reveal how high my heart was jumping inside me. I felt the same way and believed God had answered my prayers through this confirming statement by Doug!

Mac and Melissa

I first met Mac while visiting a mutual friend, Jim, in the hospital. Jim was fighting what ended up to be a losing battle with cancer. Mac walked into the hospital room. He was introduced to me and said he lived in Mount Sterling and knew about our new church plant. I invited him to come. He politely declined, saying he was attending another local church.

Our church did many outreach events to bless the community. One such effort was a nine-volt battery distribution to the whole town in the fall—the perfect time for people to change batteries in their smoke detectors. We did that distribution and Mac noticed the effort.

He and his wife, Melissa, received a battery, read the Sterling Grace blurb, and decided not to visit Sterling Grace. Instead, they decided to visit Southwest Grace in Grove City, 15 miles away. This was the church I was pastoring and was the connecting church to Sterling Grace.

Mac and Melissa came to Southwest Grace because our friend, Jim, did lose his battle with cancer, but went to be with Jesus in his death. Southwest Grace held Jim's funeral, which Mac attended. Mac and Melissa attended the church for a year or so and began visiting Sterling Grace on occasional Sunday evenings.

God was working. One evening Mac and Melissa had invited Cathy and me over for supper. We decided to throw caution to the wind and pitched a wild idea to Mac. I asked him if perhaps God was stirring his heart to become Sterling Grace's pastor/elder. He said the most interesting thing: "I thought you were going to ask that. Melissa and I have been talking and praying about this and believe God wants just such a thing!"

Cathy and I were blown away again at God's work! Pastor Mac has been leading Sterling Grace for a couple of years and is doing a great job. Doug is gathering and doing a great job as well. Mac, a full-time newspaper reporter, pastors the church with the rest of his time. Doug, formerly a waiter at Ben and Joy's restaurant, finished his degree and is now a licensed counselor in a community south of Mount Sterling. Both serve Jesus as followers of Him. Jesus has formed a dynamic, growing new church in Mount Sterling.

Why All This?

I tell that story because it is what Jesus used to help me understand how I can implement a very old idea. The gatherer/shepherd/elder church starting process is not new, but it is new to me and I am thrilled. The only thing different here is our attempt to have the simple concepts of the process molded to our culture.

When I ask how to best plant a church in a small town, a micropolitan area, or even a metropolitan area, in an economy such as ours, I get just one answer: GSE. My hope is to unpack the basic concepts of the GSE process so that you, too, can use many of these principles where you live.

GSE is primarily a church starting process. I also view it as a model in that it has basic components, which are easy to emulate, communicate and reproduce--foundational to all model approaches. But the greater value of GSE relates to its connection to a *church starting process*. So in this book, I will call it by both terms--a process and a model.

GSE is a process in that, by using it, you are not predetermining the final church's outcome. In the field, I have seen Jesus bring forth missional communities of various sizes, as well as missional attractional churches. I see it as a model in that the roles are clear and easy to follow. I do not have to redefine what the roles or terms are. They assist in ease of reproduction.

Jesus' Church

I am not a gifted evangelist. I wish I were, but I am not. I am gifted in discipling people and have been doing that for a lifetime. God does amazing things. He has taken me from being content to disciple people in the local church context to having a burden for reaching unchurched/unsaved people in a regional context. God has done this without giving me a personal evangelism gift to do so. If I were a gifted evangelist, I would take all the responsibility on myself and share Jesus with people and see some saved. Since I do not have this gift, I've been compelled to find other solutions. I needed help!

God forced me to see new churches as the way to reach people. Jesus makes it clear that His church is the perfect way to reach people (Matthew 16, 28). It is the perfect place for unsaved people to get saved and to become obedient, healthy followers of Jesus. That all happens in the local church!

This is one of many reasons to plant new churches. There is much to do!

Options

There are many ways to birth a new church, including the founding pastor model. I love it when there are many ways to get the job done. This gives us the fruit of creativity to enhance the missional work that lies before us.

The GSE process is a simple, age-old, cost-effective approach. Simply put, a gatherer gathers people to form the core group and works alongside a shepherd to begin the new church. In time, the group prays for God to raise up an elder or pastor to take the work long-term for missional penetration into the target area.

Church Birthing Models

Several models are being used in church-planting circles in North America. I am enumerating only three to compare to the GSE process. These examples, particularly the founding pastor model, are common in our region, Midwest USA.

The Apostolic Harvest Church Planter

The apostolic harvest church planter is one person who is able to go to various locations and begin churches in those locations. These planters are able to raise leaders from the harvest to carry on the church's development. The planter then moves on to repeat the process.[1]

Founding Pastor

The founding pastor model sends a church planter family to a location where they move forward to plant a church.[2] This approach requires initial funding so that the planter and his family have means to live as they start the church. Expenses include salary, benefits, core group gathering expenses, and initial set-up costs. The founding pastor model has at least two options. The founding pastor can be on the field with a team of families who either relocate with the pastor or already live there, or he can be on the field alone without a team for initial support.

Team Planting

In this model, a team of families comes together and works together to plant the church.[3] The pastor or primary leader is not necessarily known ahead of time. This form of planting has many opportunities, depending on the composition of the group.

The GSE (Gatherer/Shepherd/Elder) Key Process Characteristics

Instead of placing a founding pastor in a city from day one, with considerable financial cost, I am suggesting the use of the GSE process. The gatherer's job is to make contacts and give invitations to people who live in the town. The shepherd works in combination with the gatherer to found the church. As these two work in tandem, the group grows and is ready for a biblically qualified pastor to be placed on the field.

The model is connected, missional, and has non-Sunday morning beginning points.

"Connected" means this new church has an association with an established church that is, preferably, nearby. Connection involves more than financial consideration, since this process does not require much money (if any) to begin. More important are prayer, coaching support, and encouragement. I use the term "mother church" in those situations where financial resources are involved. For situations in which financial resources are not involved, I use the term "connected."

The second characteristic of this model is *missional*. According to Ed Stetzer, to be missional means to "plant a church that's part of the culture you're seeking to reach."[4] This is a critical assignment. The GSE process helps to pursue this idea especially if the gatherer lives in the area he or she is reaching and knows the people and the culture.

The third characteristic, "non-Sunday morning beginning points," is important for at least two reasons.

First, the issue of connection is more effective when the new church does not meet at the same time as the connecting church. This has important implications. It allows people who are involved in the new church opportunity to share with others on Sunday mornings when they meet with their church family. It allows those in the new church to have a place to tell their "story" of what God has done during the week. It keeps prayer support high and keeps the age-old "out of sight-out of mind" concept from coming true. It also allows the connecting church to see that it can plant a new church and not have to "lose" anyone right away or at all.

Second, the micropolitan communities we are reaching tend to have a preconception of Sunday morning church. An alternative option is interesting and refreshing. Though moving to Sunday morning is eventually necessary and effective in the Midwest, beginning points other than Sunday morning are very helpful.

GSE Ministry Process Benefits and Expectations

The Gatherer's Job

Church planting is eternally life changing. That is why we do it. In this simple and cost effective model, definitions are important because lives are at stake for all eternity. How to best describe a gatherer's job? I like using values, mission, and vision as categories. His work has implications well beyond the beginning work of the new church.

Gatherers' Values

The values that best describe gatherers include:

1. They have an unquenchable burden for the lost. Listen to them. What do you hear them say?

2. They have social views and values similar to those of the community they are reaching.

3. They are willing to form a close relationship with a coach in the church plant process. This relationship is key. The coach can either be a formal coach focusing on skill development, or can be a more regional person. When a group has someone with regional impact in an apostolic role, then the GSE process works much better.

4. They are team players. They see the difference between gathering and shepherding for church formation purposes.

5. They express the desire to see multiple churches planted.

6. They are passionate about meeting and connecting with people: a "people magnet."

7. They express a hunger to understand God's direction in their lives.

8. They seek to have a deep understanding of the roles necessary to form a new church in this model.

9. They are able to take direction from a supervisor/coach in well-communicated roles.

Gatherers' Vision and Mission

Gatherers must also have developed—with the help of a coach or in their own heart—an appropriate vision and mission for their core gathering work. In the founding pastor model, a core group is defined as:

> "A unified and hard-working team of believers and serious seekers committed to the leadership and vision of the church planter who are willing to sacrifice their time, use their gifts, and share their resources to reach out to their chosen community in order to win the lost and gather a healthy Christian congregation."[5]

Adapted to the GSE process we can express it this way:

A core group is a unified and hard-working team of believers and serious seekers committed to the *vision and mission of the gathering team* who are willing to sacrifice their time, use their gifts and share their resources to reach out to their chosen community in order to win the lost and gather a healthy Christian congregation.

The gatherer's mission is to be the initial key person in the beginning stages of dozens of core group gatherings for newly formed churches in a region.

How Do I Find a Gatherer?

You may ask, "Well, how do I find a gatherer? How do I know if I am one?" Great questions. Here is a simple exercise that may help identify gatherers in your world:

Please read the following statements and do not try to analyze them. Simply allow the statement/question to bring up the names and faces of people. As this happens, write down the names:

1. First person who greets someone new in your church or in your business.

2. Someone you are meeting with in a public place; you get a little bothered that you cannot have a conversation with him or her because so many people are talking to him or her.

3. Someone in a business that is public oriented, for example:
    • salesperson
    • marketer
    • entrepreneur

4. An extrovert or a very people-oriented person.

5. Someone with whom you share the GSE vision and gatherer's role. If you share this vision and role, and he says yes, you have one.

6. When you are in a public place and see someone who fits this description, approach him and sell the GSE vision.

7. The person in the church that you are having the most trouble with in the church when it comes to modalic thinking or "regular" church thinking.

Sodalic/Modalic

The words "sodalic and modalic" are both fairly new terms in being used here in North America. They have been missionary or missional terms used to describe missional efforts in other lands. As the state of our own need has grown to be so self evident, we now use these terms to describe our situation.

Ralph Winter drew attention to these concepts in 1973. In an article summarizing his comments at a summit, he said:

> "In order to speak conveniently about the continuing similarities in function, let us now call the synagogue and diocese *modalities*, and the missionary band and monastery *sodalities*. Elsewhere I have developed these terms in detail, but briefly, a modality is a structured fellowship in which there is no distinction of sex or age, while a sodality is a structured fellowship in which membership involves an adult

(continued on next page)

---

second decision beyond modality membership, and is limited by either age or sex or marital status. In this use of these terms, both the *denomination* and the *local congregation* are modalities, while a mission agency or a local men's club are sodalities."[6]

Both terms are wonderful and healthy. In short, for our purposes, modalic is used to describe all that is involved to build, keep and maintain health in a local church context. This is a focus on the 99 sheep that are not lost and what we must do to keep their environment healthy so they can grow and continue to follow Jesus in new and amazing ways.

Sodalic is used to describe all that is involved in going someplace we have not yet gone. This is a focus on the one sheep that is lost and all that is necessary to find and save that one sheep. We do not live in a 99 percent Christian world while only needing to seek one percent.

Sodalic efforts are those described by words like "sent, sending, go, going, mission, missional, network etc." One of the keys is for us to see both terms as healthy and necessary – both are good. But, one tends to not understand the other! Modalically focused people tend to not care a whole lot about the mission "out there" because their love, focus and energy is on the mission to build and keep health in the place where they are plugged into their church. Sodalically minded people pass out quickly in board meetings, group meetings that deal with maintaining good, necessary things. But get them outside the room or outside the church building – wow!

8. Someone who knows "everyone."

9. A person in your church in whom you see great potential; you also have seasons of great disappointment in him or her because he or she has not engaged or "risen" to the level you had hoped.

10. Everyone can invite someone to a gathering. Who would you like to do that inviting? Who would you like to work with in a gathering GSE work?

11. Someone who is seeing some amazing transformation with/from Jesus Christ in their life – they are a prime gatherer!

12. Who are you comfortable targeting with transformational concepts to see Jesus do amazing things in them? They are now your gatherer.

With your list of names, you can begin praying and sharing this vision of a GSE process.

From these values, vision, and mission we can articulate a goal-based, conceptual progression for the gatherer. His or her work can move through three stages:

1. He or she is present in the community.

2. He or she makes contacts in the community.

3. He or she works with a shepherd to gather a core group.

The Ministry of Presence

In this phase of the work, the gatherer's mere presence becomes the first step in beginning the church birthing process. In this phase, the rest of the plan can be clarified. If the gatherer is already well known in the community, his or her ministry of presence is already formed and the task is simplified. Have lunch or breakfast with the gatherer in his or her community and observe what happens. If you experience many interruptions during the meal, it's a very good sign! I know I am in the presence of a gatherer when I am in a public place, such as a restaurant, and he or she is speaking to people and people are speaking to him or her.

Another way to express this is: When a person goes into a gas station and it takes them 10 minutes to get coffee and come back to the vehicle, you are likely in the presence of a gatherer.

A ministry of presence is best seen in Jesus. He was the master of ministering "where He was." So often Jesus was walking and people came up to Him or He engaged them—all because He was there. He was present.

If the gatherer is not from the city he or she is targeting, then his or her job is to establish a ministry of presence. This can be done through many venues.

The Gatherer's Contact-Making Strategy in the Community

The gatherer, if already known in the community, can create a list of 25 families with whom he or she can attempt to share the church-planting vision. He or she can then carve out two time slots during the week in which to meet with these families and share the concept of a new church. It is important that the gatherer meets with his coach and shepherd (if available) to form this plan. The shepherd's role is also important, as will soon be evident.

The gatherer continues the time-sensitive and pressure-filled work of networking with contacts in the community. It is a process of engaging and sharing the vision of the new church with the contacts developed. This process may or may not bring many families initially to the core group formation, but in the long term, it brings a valuable dividend.

A gatherer recently told about a family he had invited to his church gathering more than a year ago. Another person also invited this family and now they are beginning to attend their church. The gatherer re-invited the family a few other times in the last year, but God worked and brought the family, it seems, at someone else's invitation. There is nothing wrong with any of this. It is all God's work!

Core Group Gathering with the Aid of the Shepherd

As the process moves along, families who have expressed interest must come together. It's important to form regular worship meetings and use this worship time as core group formation. Three families, not counting the gatherer's and shepherd's families, are the initial goal for the church to "come alive." We use this term to describe when a church begins. We prefer to use a metric that involves the number of families, rather than a specific number of attendees. We have chosen three as a key number to begin with—three families coming together to help form a new church is when the church is a church. It "comes alive" at that time.

The shepherd initiates the core group meetings and worship services. He shoulders the primary work of the worship service, which should be simple when the group begins meeting. Meanwhile, the gatherer continues to make contacts. The coach teams with the gatherer and the shepherd.

There are at least three key roles involved at this very early stage: gatherer, shepherd, and coach. We have described the gatherer and his or her work. He or she should not be distracted from what Jesus designed him or her to do. The shepherd is the one who helps provide biblical care for the families coming together and oversees the formation of the worship services. These services are meant to be simple in their beginning. The coach is also key. This person is either a pure coach or perhaps the regional key "apostolic" type person who is assisting in the region for this work. This person can be both the apostolic oversight person and the coach.

The two key transitions that have the greatest potential for failure in this process are: 1) The transition from the gatherer doing his or her work to the combination of gatherer and shepherd working as a team. The regional impact person or apostle-type person and/or coach can work most effectively in this transition; 2) the transition to an elder/pastor on the field as the church grows.

This transition from gatherer and shepherd working together to adding the elder is also assisted most effectively by the same apostolic-type person and/or coach. This person needs to stay attuned to the group dynamics. Is the elder a known person? If so, then the transition is easier; if not, more work is needed to communicate clearly what is happening and why.

Gatherer/Shepherd/Elder Process

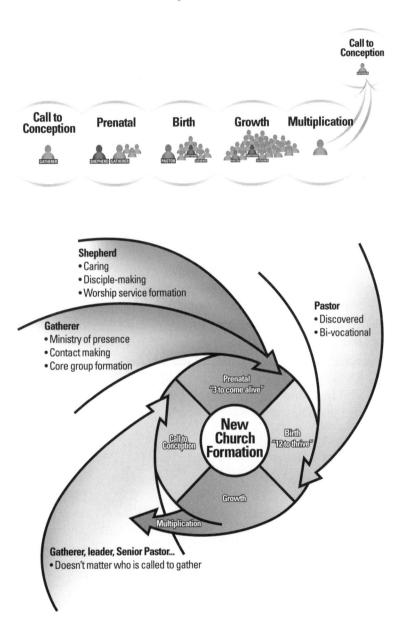

Phase Development of the Gathering Process

It is critical that we develop and understand the ministry process of the gatherer (see chart). This process is also keyed into initial phase development in the prenatal phase work. In the core gathering process of the prenatal phase, picture three differing engagements. These three differing engagements are meant to help measure the group's movement from a collection of people to a number of families who are committed to becoming a new church. The work described here is all part of the core gathering process in the prenatal phase and is what the gatherer is working toward with the shepherd and coach.

The shepherd can come on point for this process and the coach can help as the process continues. The process described here is this: Engage a Discovery Group process; move to a Seed Group time; end with a Launch Team process.

Discovery Group: In the Discovery Group phase, the families that have been initially gathered need to go through a discovery process to find out whether God wants them to plant a new church. This phase addresses the "if" question. Are we going to plant a church? If we are going to plant a new church, what do we need to address carefully?

I believe Jesus has already answered the question: "Should we plant another church?" This process focuses more on this question: "Should we be the team that comes together to plant this new church?" "If Jesus desires a new church here in our town, are we the ones He wants to do this?" If the group answers "yes" to the question of the discovery process, then we move on to the Seed Group.

Here is the discovery process that helps us arrive at a decision and addresses these topics:

1. Church birthing - Acts 17:1-9 and 1 Thessalonians 1
2. Congregational DNA - Acts 2:41-47;
3. Lost things - Luke 15:1-31;
4. God's call - Acts 13:1-5 and 16:4-10;
5. Spiritual warfare - Ephesians 6:10-20.

Seed Group: The Seed Group phase is made up of a small group of Discovery Group graduates who are willing to continue meeting to pray about the formation of a new church. The Seed Group can be a collecting point for graduates from a sequence of Discovery Groups. The meetings should include specific prayer concerning the starting of a new church, an open time of vision discovery and discussion, and some very light spiritual formation activities.

Seed Group work involves more specific training, whether it is gatherer training, greater training on the GSE concepts, or other areas. Also valuable at this phase is general spiritual formation activity—the more as a team, the better.

Launch Team: This phase now addresses the foregone conclusion. Since we are planting and we have a good size group, "then" we can now move on in more intentional development of ourselves as a church family. The three major systems to be addressed at this point are shepherding or people care, children's ministries, and worship.[7]

Church-planting experts agree that whatever the *form* chosen for the new church plant, the development of a substantial, cohesive, and committed Core Group/Launch Team is the most important human factor in the success and health of the new congregation.

A Core Group/Launch Team is NOT:

• A Bible study
• A group of inquirers
• A collection of disgruntled church attendees
• A gathering of spiritual seekers
• A church split or splinter group
• People who like and are committed to the church planter.

A true Core Group/Launch Team may grow out of any or all of these groups, but it is, by definition and necessity, much more.

A church-planting Core Group/Launch Team is a unified, hardworking team of believers and serious seekers committed to the leadership and vision of the church planter. They are willing to sacrifice their time, use their gifts, and share their resources to reach out to their chosen community in order to win the lost and gather a healthy Christian congregation.

Key Characteristics

1. Team
2. Unified
3. Hard-working
4. Believers
5. Serious seekers
6. Committed
7. Leadership and vision of the church-planter
8. Willing to sacrifice
9. Willing to use their gifts
10. Willing to share resources
11. Reaching out
12. Winning
13. Gathering
14. A healthy Christ-centered congregation[8]

Notes

[1]Stetzer, *Planting Missional Churches,* 53-54.

[2]Ibid, 61-69.

[3]Ibid, 70-75.

[4]Ibid, 1.

[5]Terry Hofecker, "Seminar on North American Church Planting" (syllabus, Grace Theological Seminary, Winona Lake, Ind., March 6-10, 2006).

[6]Ralph Winter, "The Two Structures of God's Redemptive Mission," *Foundations of the World Christian Movements: A Larger Perspective,* (Pasadena, Calif.: Institute of International Studies, 2008), 223-224.

[7]Terry Hofecker, VO Ministry Team conversation, March 2010.

[8]Hofecker, Terry. "Seminar on North American Church Planting," (unpublished syllabus, Ashland Theological Seminary, Ashland, Ohio, March 2006).

Chapter 2

Simple, Age-Old, Highly-Efficient and Cost-Effective

FURTHER DEVELOPMENT
OF GSE PROCESS

*"Faith... is the art of holding on to things your reason
once accepted, despite your changing moods."*
C. S. Lewis

*"Faith is much better than belief. Belief is when
someone else does the thinking."*
Richard Fuller

*"The greatest act of faith is when a man
understands he is not God."*
Oliver Wendell Homes, Jr.

Church birthing needs are obvious everywhere in America. A biotic model is normally chosen to explain the process of church planting. Bob Logan explains the phases of the biotic model of church planting.

The gatherer and shepherd's work
are primary tools in the prenatal phase
of church development.

The first phase is conception. This phase deals with all the tasks that need to be accomplished before actually beginning the process of planting the new church.[1] Matters developed here include, among other concerns: call confirmation in the heart of the planter, initial assessment of the planter, and completion of the vision documents and vision process.

The second phase is the prenatal phase, which is considered the most important.[2] More church plant failures can be traced to failures in this phase than any other.[3] This phase involves various approaches to core group gathering. In the VisionOhio Operations Center, we use "five families to come alive (as a church) and 25 to thrive (go public with the new church)" when considering a founding pastor model.[4]

The gatherer needs to work through the "call to conception" phase in his or her own heart. The gatherer also has the most impact in the prenatal phase. Common barriers in the core-gathering phase are of critical concern to this process.

Common plateaus in the early phases of the work occur at five, 15, and 35. Hence, we would need to change our metric in this micropolitan model to "three to come alive and 12 to thrive." This would translate into three families in the core group (not including the gatherer's and shepherd's families) and build to 12 families for a public launch service.

With the time and energy limitations of an unpaid gatherer, this growth can be best called *moderate*. It is very important to hold expectations in check for this part of the new church development. The shepherd's work on the field would assist the gatherer, but the shepherd would have limited impact on contact-making with the gatherer. God's choice of His pastor for this newly-birthed church would most likely be the key to growth to the 12-family level.

Shepherd's Work

The shepherd's job, simply expressed, is to provide spiritual care for the gatherer, as well as for the people who are gathered into the core group. The value the shepherd brings to the work is keeping the gatherer freed up to keep the contact-making an on-going process. As families are connected to the core group, spiritual needs will grow. The gatherer must be kept free from "meeting" these shepherding needs, so he or she can focus on his or her unique gift of connecting with people not yet in the church. If his work of contact-making is consumed in shepherd work, *then the church fails to develop*. This point is critical to development, and the coach involved in the work must also understand this point.

The shepherd's job includes, but is not limited to:

1. Worship service formation and engagement;

2. Worship service development and advancement;

3. Shepherding care provided for those already in the new church;

4. Discipleship matters engaged for growth and obedience to Jesus;

5. Service opportunities as a church family – prayer walks, ministry of presence matters etc.;

6. Core group formation issues covered through the connection to a coach;

7. Extensive prayer connection to a region.

Benefits and Expectations Involved in the GSE Process

The GSE process has many benefits. I share some of these benefits here (further developed later in the book) to help form and mold key expectations in our hearts. These expectations are necessary for regional implementation. If we do not understand these benefits and expectations, we broadly underestimate the impact of this simple process. Consider the benefits this process brings and how they can mold our expectations to impact our various regions.

Greater Lay Involvement

We are able to see more people from our church families involved in the ready and white harvest. We are better able to direct men and women to this powerful work of birthing new churches in our regions.

"In order for the Gospel to go somewhere, a messenger had to carry it. And wherever messengers went with it, we see churches established. Thus, we have the many letters of the New Testament written not to believers in Corinth, Ephesus, or Thessalonica but to churches gathered in those places."[5]

Moderate Growth

We are able to experience moderate growth for our new churches. Though family growth numerically is solely the work of God, it is important that we have expectations of moderate growth in the newly-birthed churches in this process and allow our hearts to accept this as normal. It is counter-current press, counter-current church culture; but we need to examine our thinking here.

Mark Chaves reports: "The median congregation has only 75 regularly participating people and an annual budget of approximately $90,000. Ninety percent of all congregations have 350 or fewer people. While mega churches and fast-growing churches grab headlines, they are comparatively few in number. Mega churches, defined as congregations with average attendance of 2,000 or more adults and children, represent 0.4 percent of the total Protestant church population (although they draw almost 10 percent of all worshipers). We like mega churches—well, many of them! But we believe they are but one possible solution to reaching our culture for Christ. Ultimately, we need far more churches than we currently have in order to reach our ever-expanding and diversifying culture. Among churches of all sizes, growing churches are rare."[6]

Small Churches

We are able to see the value of small or smaller churches in our region. Moderate growth also breeds the necessity of small churches in our region as a result of the use of this process. May God develop these, His churches, at His will and speed. The overriding goal of any church-birthing movement is the starting of new churches. The overall health of each church is of extreme importance, but the key is the starting of new churches. More healthy churches are not going to come into existence without the extensive planting of new churches.

What traits do we use as markers of health? Whether we use Christian Schwartz' list or George Bullard's list, we come away with vital small groups, holistic worship, leadership development, etc. When we take the time to figure out what makes these traits effective in a group of Christians, we see these traits are also key in birthing

26

new churches. The best way for us to radically remake our culture and meet the needs of people all around us is to start new churches.

I just hung up from a phone call in which the man I was talking to was asking me if there was a particular church (of our denomination) in a certain city location. I thought for a moment and then said, "No, we do not have a church there." But then I said, "But we long for and dream for the day when new churches are started and I know nothing about them!" That is a day to long for—a church a day in our region!

"At the one-year mark, average attendance of a new church is 41 people. At the two-year mark, it's 56. At the three-year mark, it's 73. At the four-year mark, it's 84."[7]

My point is simply this: research shows us that even with full-time energy in a church plant—the full time energy is defined by the funding provided—church attendance reaches 84 by year four. Studies show that a church typically plateaus in attendance by year 15; by year 35 this same church has trouble replacing the members it loses.[8]

Peter Drucker said, "Bigger is better turned out to be another Twentieth Century myth."[9]

"Leaders like it big, but people like it small (in the context of a worship service)."[10] Browning goes on to say:

"Sid Porter says, 'If you want 1,000 pounds of meat, raise elephants. If you want 1,000 tons of meat, raise rabbits.' If you put two elephants in a room and two rabbits in a room, in three years you will have three elephants and 476 million rabbits."[11]

Perhaps we can allow ourselves to become comfortable with an explosive growth curve of churches as we think in terms of rabbits and all the limits that "rabbit thinking" brings on – the mess, the smell, the food consumption. But we can also see the sheer number of rabbits that came through a natural process.

Regional Connection

We are able to see connection with a regional church. In this process, we need to see the newly-birthed churches connected with an established church in the region. This established church provides necessary encouragement and prayer support.

Can a new church be started with this GSE Process without a connected church? Yes, it can. Can it be started without regional, apostolic connection? Good question. It would be hard. Encouragement is a key part to this process. Discouragement is high among church planters and gatherers. Regional, apostolic types, as well as focused, non-directive coaches, are best solutions available to us today. The ink in the Christian press is given to the fast-growing and high-numbered churches. All church workers and planters long for this (large, fast-growing plants), but it is given to just a few.

Cost-Effective Model Process

We are able to see a cost-effective process for planting new churches. This model has a clear advantage for church planting because it does not require large sums of money to get the church planting process started and new churches birthed. Financial assistance is not the center of the process. Focus on a bi-vocational pastor allows the church to grow to levels as the church itself develops.

This factor is a key consideration. As we are able to train local church leaders on how to implement this church-planting process, imagine the impact when finances are removed from the table. Imagine the freedom that moves into the hearts of local church leaders as they brainstorm about communities they are burdened to reach for Jesus Christ by a new church!

"Highly Efficient" Process

We are able to see the value of "highly efficient energy" investment for birthing new churches. "Highly efficient energy" is the term I use to describe the work of the gatherer and shepherd in a non-paid assignment. This is made clearer by visualizing the amount of time and energy a full-time, founding pastor is able to invest in the pre-natal work of the church. In this process, the same energy is not possible.

A couple of years ago, our 40-year-old furnace went out the week of Christmas. Our old furnace was no more than 40 percent efficient. We replaced it with an 80 percent efficient furnace. The salesman said the difference is how much energy or heat the furnace loses while it is making and distributing the heat. If I understood him right, my old furnace's 40 percent efficient system was allowing 60 percent of the heat produced to escape through the chimney!

The more efficient the furnace, the better it is for me and my family. The more efficient the furnace, the less expensive it is, and the better it runs. This is also true in church planting. The more efficient the model, the better. The more efficient the model, the less expensive it is. We want efficient models, especially in this day. The GSE is one of those.

Reproduction

We are able to see the GSE's ability to reproduce itself. This process, in its simple expression, is simple to reproduce. Whether through an established church or through other means, when a gatherer is identified (either self-identified or identified by another person), that person can begin the work. Shepherds seem to abound in established churches. Those who are able to shepherd small groups are easily able to provide the care necessary in the initial core-gathering work in the prenatal phase. Vision, desire, and passion are the necessary components for the reproduction of this process on a large scale. Imagine a man who pastors an established church, with the passion to reach others in his community or region, connecting with a gatherer who lives in a community or part of town he desires to reach.

Use of Spiritual gifts

As a pastor, I have always dreamed of the day when there is a more diverse involvement of spiritually gifted people. We are looking for gifted gatherers and shepherds. Using the character traits described earlier, we can identify gifted gatherers. Gifted shepherds seem to abound in my denomination.

Coaching

As stated earlier, the most obvious weaknesses of this approach are the key transitions. The first transition occurs when the gatherer and shepherd team up together. If they are not able to work well together, the work is compromised and most likely will not survive. This transition is less vulnerable than the second one, but we need to pay attention to it as it begins. The second key transition occurs when the initial core group of potentially three to seven families transitions from the shepherd to the elder/pastor on the field.

The coach is key to making these vital transitions work. The coach needs to understand the transitions. He also needs to understand the varied roles of the gatherer and shepherd. The coach works with the gatherer and shepherd on the field; his influence is critical because of the highly efficient energy and moderate growth possibilities. The coach must also be carefully in tune with the discouragement factor of the gatherer and shepherd. Good coaching is necessary.

Simple Concepts in the GSE Process

Some of the "simple" parts of the GSE process are enumerated below.

Small Churches

Church planting in America has many outcomes. We hear most about the success stories of incredibly large growth cycles culminating in very large churches. Though these examples of God's gracious work are glorious and wonderful, can we expect that as our norm? No, we cannot. The average size of a church in America today is 75.[12] How often do we talk in glorious terms about a church plant growing to 75? Yet God's work in the world often generates a church of 40.[13] I am defining a small church as being between three and 75 people in attendance in the largest gathering the church has.

It is not for personal reasons or the making of excuses that we talk about small churches. It is dealing with the reality of God's work today. As we ask God for a church multiplication movement in our region, we must acknowledge that the fruit of His work in the world is normally a small church.[14]

We must also understand that Stetzer tells us there are not any church multiplication movements in any of the 34 industrialized nations in the world.[15] What does this mean? It means we are not going to see a large church movement of new churches in our region.

Multiplication movements in the world today are producing small churches.[16]

In my opinion, we hunger for large churches in America. We commonly use attendance of 200 as a measuring stick, though a better measure might be 150.[17] The two numbers are actually the same when gauging relationships within the church.

The issues that create the barrier at the 150 mark are real. Ultimately, the greatest issue is one of expectations. Some report that unless the new church grows to more than 200 in the first two years, there will be problems that will keep the church from growing and being effective.[18] Others feel they are fighting to keep the church going if they serve in a church with fewer than 200 in attendance.[19] Schaller, Wagner, and Malphurs echo similar ideas.[20]

So what does all this mean? In church-planting circles, it seems we have arrived at the place where we need to be more specific and candid in our conversations and how we discuss numbers. Gray is clear and honest when he indicates he is talking about planting churches in metropolitan areas.[21] To be clear on the environment of the church plant is important. In smaller towns, the small church is just as powerful—if not more so—than a large church.[22]

God has "never been constrained to work through the many rather than the few."[23] Perhaps humility is the key to the small church. Since God has limited the growth of His churches in the world to smaller sizes, how can we best connect with this divine reality? I can argue all day about the beauty of the small church as demonstrated by God in the world or in America. But what is the point? Who am I trying to convince?

It may be easy to overlook the matters in which small churches excel. For example, the bigger a church grows, the less effective it becomes "both in quality and in its capability to reach new people for Christ."[24] A recent study does point out two matters in which small, established churches do not excel: planning and process improvement.[25] While my point about the value of the small church is related to the initial work of planting, I recognize a small church plant is likely to remain small. Kelly's study shows the need to address the two critical points of planning and process improvement. Church planters can plan well and have connection to process improvement. They are tied to process improvement mostly through their own training, but also through the support network a healthy church planter can access.

When it comes to poor planning and process improvement, another weakness or reason why this occurs is related to the bi-vocational work of a GSE worker. As the GSE works itself out, the leadership development work is in need of clear delineation of leadership as the church develops. These transitions are important to note, and the coach can help in all this.

All of this leads to an important distinction related to a small church and its formation and beginning stages. Most materials criticizing small church are addressing established churches, and typically those established churches are farther along in their life cycles. If a detailed study shows planning and process improvement to be key, and if church planters have possible access to tools to assist this development in their plant, then perhaps the missional nature of their ministry can continue. A small church with a missional or mission focus is a powerful church.

Another issue to mention in this section on small churches is active versus passive worship. All church plant and established church goals are one-fold: to produce obedient, multiplying disciples. Both large and small churches can do this. The more common form of worship service is the general gathering of all the people in that church at one place and one time—Sunday morning for example. The average worship service, regardless whether a small church or large, has a high potential for passive worship, which may not be specifically defined as worship at all.[26]

The goal is active worship on the part of all participants physically present at a gathering. Most leaders passionately desire their "flock" to engage God actively in a powerful, worshipful service. Can a small church accomplish this more easily and effectively? Can a church plant do this more easily and effectively? I believe it can.

Moderate Growth Concepts

Moderate growth in church planting. What a thought! How can I endorse such a concept? Am I lowering the standards for church growth so there are no defeats and no hurt feelings? No. Moderate growth is a concept I am not finding in the current literature, but which is necessary to consider in the GSE process.

Gray, Sjogren, Wagner, Schaller, and Martin are proponents of doing everything possible to move through the 200 barrier and develop a church of that size as quickly as possible.[27] When professional church planters are involved, moderate growth is normally not an option. Moderate growth churches by professional planters are deemed failures.[28]

Some of the moderate growth concepts I propose are predicated upon the most simple of directives. John 20:21, "As the Father has sent me, I also send you (NASB)." The exchange of citizenship from this earth to God's kingdom is the order of the day. If our desire is either to rule the world or to withdraw from it, we miss our mark.[29] If our desire is to meet the missional example and call of Jesus, we do well.

To keep my missional focus, the amount of growth to expect remains in God's hands. Moderate growth has advantages over the time in which the growth occurs. God tends to allow us to move through growth cycles, then assimilation cycles. Though we typically do not experience numeric growth during assimilation cycles, they are fascinating times nonetheless.

Hirsch talks about a matter he calls the missional leader's job: moving a system toward the edge of chaos, that is, to become highly responsive to its environment.[30] Movement such as this is obtainable in any church, regardless of size. Can a moderate growth process facilitate this type of movement to missional connection in community, which breeds chaos and provides movement toward chaos? Chaos is good, especially in church work. The more sedentary the church, the more programmed and predictable it is, and the farther from chaos it is. We tend to applaud safety and programming. We need to stop applauding and instead rejoice in the discomfort chaos can bring, as long as the chaos is brought to us through missional connection to the mission field. Chaos is helpful if it is brought to us because we are getting involved in the lives of people who need to know Jesus Christ.

What if we are able to make "failure" more palatable and less expensive financially? What if we are able to lower the risk and see what God might do? Malphurs is right when he talks openly about failure. Most of us hate failure, and we do not attempt big things for God because we are afraid we might fail. After all, what might others think?[31] What if this GSE process lowers the risk factor enough for greater risk in church planting? Is that something pleasing to our Lord? I believe it is.

Malphurs argues that a church needs to have at least 50 people before it can birth a new church.[32] He later states the need to reach the size of 200 as soon as possible. It seems we continue to focus on a church of 200.

The best way to communicate moderate growth as an important consideration in the GSE process is to tie it to the highly efficient energy idea. More people identify with the obvious fact that a few hours a week have one impact and full-time involvement has another impact. The difference between a planter working full-time and a planter/gatherer working part-time or even just a few hours is what I am calling "highly efficient energy."

Highly Efficient Energy Concepts

Highly efficient energy is the reality that comes from a bi-vocational gatherer. It is what happens when the gatherer already works a full-time job and plants a church in the remaining time.

No one in ministry disparages a person who does all he/she can do to share the gospel of Jesus Christ with someone. However, we do not make it a strategy—something to shoot for or to plan for—as a positive tool in church planting. I believe we need to remedy this as soon as possible. We must establish highly efficient energy as an acceptable and specific plan for planting churches. This all ties into the next category and our expectations.

Greater Visionary Involvement

Can a non-professional plant a church? Most will say, "Yes." Do we provide a venue for them to do so? I am not sure that we do. There is always a role on the team. But there is not an available role to lead the team. As long as church planting remains a job for professionals, non-professionals will not participate. We must continue to find ways to make the work of church planting as compelling as possible.

Permission-giving systems or structures are what we are seeking. Stetzer tells us that the need for permission-giving structures is key to our future engagement of movements of new churches.[33]

The issue of greater visionary involvement relates to the regular church attendee or "pew sitter." Schwarz shows that in the small church with fewer than 100 in attendance, 31 percent are practicing their spiritual gifts. In a church with attendance over 1,000, 17 percent are practicing their spiritual gifts.[34] Schwarz shows how a smaller church can more easily implement a gifted gatherer into the church planting work.

As we make the vision part of church planting more available to the normal church attendee, we appropriate powerful tools that aid us in planting churches in micropolitan areas.

Failures

We all have shared, said, and believed this statistic: three out of five new church plants fail. Some even share that only 20 percent survive. Leadership Network numbers indicate a different story. Ninety-two percent of new churches make it to their second anniversary and 68 percent are still in existence after year four.[35]

This may mean that the systems being used are working to help bring greater health to new churches. Of all the factors that influence the health and life of a new plant, perhaps Jesus Christ has given to us ways to see this all happen. Perhaps now is the time to take advantage of the progression and increase a more acceptable view of risk and how to manage it. When we consider that smaller church size pleases Jesus Christ through the efforts of our dear folks who are part of our churches, then we are well on our way!

> "Our caution about big churches is that the more they grow, the more likely they are to grow by addition rather than multiplication. It is never easy to give up the people and resources necessary to multiply. The larger a church becomes the

greater the temptation becomes to take on a sedentary position to movemental Christianity. The larger the church, the less able it is to multiply itself—unless its leaders continually make heroes of small replicable groups, teams, or classes. In reality, a church grows bigger by doing small better."[36]

Notes

[1]Logan and Ogne, *Churches Planting Churches*, 4-6.

[2]Ibid, 4-7.

[3]Terry Hofecker, classroom discussion, 2006.

[4]Vision Ohio, personal communication, 2007

[5]Stetzer and Bird, *Viral Churches*, 22.

[6]Ibid, 59-60.

[7]Stetzer and Bird, *Viral Churches*, 101- this study was done with church plants that had received funding in their process and progression from a funding source – report, 1

[8]Stetzer and Bird, *Viral Churches*, 26

[9]quoted in Browning, *Deliberate Simplicity*, 129

[10]Browning, *Deliberate Simplicity*, 144

[11]Ibid, 198

[12]Hartford Institute for Religion Research, http://hirr.hartsem.edu/research/fastfacts/fast_facts.html#sizecong (accessed March 5, 2013).

[13]Garrison, 17

[14]Garrison, 18

[15]Stetzer and Bird, *Viral Churches*, 167.

[16]Garrison, 24-25.

[17]Gladwell, *The Tipping Point*, 179.

[18]Gray, 39ff

[19]Sjogren, *Community of Kindness*, 169

[20]Schaller, *Looking in the Mirror*, 20; Wagner, *Church Planting for a Greater Harvest*, 128; Malphurs, *Planting Growing Churches for the 21st Century*, 66

[21]Gray, 43

[22]Gray, 134; Malphurs, *Planting Growing Churches for the 21st Century*, 66.

[23]Rowell, *Magnifying Your Vision for the Small Church*, 149.

[24]Schwarz, *The Strong Little Church*, 53.

[25]Kelly, *Study Examines Challenges Within Smaller Churches.*

[26]Hirsch, *The Forgotten Ways*, 43.

[27]for example: Gray, 39ff.

[28]Gray, 41 and 108.

[29]Saucy, "The Presence of the Kingdom and the Life of the Church," 46.

[30]Hirsch, *The Forgotten Ways*, 184.

[31]Malphurs, *Planting Growing Churches for the 21st Century*, 72-73.

[32]Ibid, 254.

[33]Stetzer and Bird, *Viral Churches*, 173, 181

[34]Schwarz, *The Strong Little Church*, 54

[35]Stetzer and Bird, *Viral Churches*, 104

[36]Ibid, 141

Chapter 3

STARTING SOMETHING NEW

"Learn from the mistakes of others.
You can't live long enough to make them all yourself."
Eleanor Roosevelt

"Success is the ability to go from one failure to another
with no loss of enthusiasm."
Sir Winston Churchhill

"Go, make disciples of all people groups . . ."
Jesus Christ

Have you ever traveled through a micropolitan town? Not the one-or-two traffic light towns, but those under 50,000 in population. As you drive through that town, do you think, "I wonder how the gospel is doing in this city?" "I wonder what it would be like to come to this city and start something?"

If so, then welcome to the club. How do we begin something new (for us) in a city we are not yet in? Though there are many ways to go about penetrating a new city, let us explore some thoughts of how to penetrate a micropolitan city for Jesus Christ. And, further, how can we penetrate a city and join with the other churches that are preaching the gospel and to reach this city for Jesus Christ?

Regardless of the final method chosen to enter a new city, it requires energy and time. Someone needs to invest energy and time to figure out the best way. Or, better yet, someone needs to invest time and exegete the community to figure out the best way to go.

Making First Contact

A couple of years ago, I was investigating Lima, Ohio, a post-industrial city with a population of approximately 38,000. I was trying to recruit a church planter to go to this city and begin a new work. On two different trips, one with a team and one without, we simply stopped into a church that had activity in its parking lot. We stopped in and talked with the staff of a Nazarene church and also with the staff of a Baptist church. Both stops were foundationally helpful.

We found out insightful information about the needs of the city. We found out methods they were trying and what was working for them and what was not. But even more important than that, we found out how welcome a new effort would be in Lima if we were to go there.

We also stopped and talked to the city planner and other city officials to find out all we could about the city. Though I was not able to find a planter to go to Lima at that time, it was helpful to see how much information was available through simple presence and questioning.

The basic idea is to go somewhere and meet people and talk to them. Invest in them and in their city and allow God to move your heart to see this city as He sees it. From this initial point, there are many options. Depending on what you have gleaned from the target city, you can then begin to form a plan. We can benefit from the work of others.

On Your Own

My favorite way to penetrate a new community is to find the local downtown restaurant. Spending time in a restaurant talking to people and watching them gives a wealth of information.

Prayer walks are also helpful in this exploratory process. I recall driving through a town of interest to me, not far from where I live. I invested an afternoon to "prayer walk" the town. As I was there walking and praying, trying to listen to God, I made a discovery.

I was walking down a residential part of this town when I came upon a building that, from a distance, looked like an old church. It had architecture like a church. I found that it *was* an old church, surrounded on all sides by houses.

40

Coming upon it, I saw that it once was a church, but had become a local business that had gone "out of business." Boarded up windows and peeling white paint was what this residential community had to see: a church that had ended, but also a business that could not keep up. As I was pondering this site, I turned to look at the house across the street. It had a sign on the front door that said something like this: "Whatever you are selling or **preaching**, I am not interested. Stay away!"

It was at this time I heard from God clearly. Someone needs to reach the family that lives in this house! God has his man there, now, doing a great work for Him!

Help From Others:

What have others done as they have penetrated micropolitan cities with a new work? Some friends have helped me, and I will share what they have experienced and practiced to get a new church going in a micropolitan city.

My friends are responding to a series of questions that will give us food for thought in starting new things. The questions posed to them were:

1. *What were the specific considerations in your heart and mind as you began a new micropolitan ministry? (What was it that drove you to do this?)*

2. *What initial steps did you take when you started your work (a new church or a need-meeting ministry)? Did you come as an insider, or as an outsider, to the community—and how did this factor into how you began?*

3. *How did you legitimize your work? Who was necessary to come on board with your vision, and how did they buy in?*

4. *What price did you pay to create this ministry?*

5. *What responses did you receive from those targeted by your newly-begun micropolitan ministry?*

6. *What specific lessons have you learned? What would you do differently?*

7. *What advice would you give to someone who was considering starting a new ministry in a micropolitan community?*

In using these questions with a series of my friends, here is a sampling of the responses:

Medina, Ohio

Concerning Medina, Ohio (population 28,000), Pastor Will Lohnes told us:

1. *What were the specific considerations in your heart and mind as you began a new micropolitan ministry? (What was it that drove you to do this?)*

    I sensed a lack in the church to get out of itself and touch the community. Christians ought and must go to the world with the Gospel of grace and not ask the world to come to us for it. They have needs that only the church can supply but we are too caught up in our programs to meet the real needs. I saw "people watching," not winning the lost. Don't get me wrong, I love a good worship and preaching service but without the seeking service from the heart outside to the world, it becomes a practical heresy: singing well doesn't mean seeking well. All said, I desired a church of precept and practical Christianity in meeting the needs of the community.

2. *What initial steps did you take when you started your work (a new church or a need-meeting ministry)? Did you come as an insider, or as an outsider, to the community—and how did this factor into how you began?*

    We started The Fountain of Grace Church in 2005 right in the middle of town where needs are most seen. I found individuals of like mind and passion, and we formed a leadership team. Our first simple step was to gain a habit of noticing and seeing the community in a new light of supplying rather than asking. It took some time, but we turned the corner when our people just wanted to help. We went to businesses and asked how we can help their business become more successful. After years of doing a multitude of things like this, we have a reputation that runs along "giving cups of water" to individuals that at times do not know they are thirsty.

I was an insider in the community for seven years before we launched. The Lord had moved my heart for evangelism rather than just exposition. Being a part of the town helped immensely in knowing the deficiencies and sufficiency's of it. I knew people, businesses, values, direction...all necessary for wise and capable leadership. Simply, we walked into a coffee shop on the town square and said, "I want to help you make this a more successful business. I will do whatever is necessary... wash windows, clean cookie sheets, sweep floors... and I know, it seems I am from Mars." After four weeks of servicing and entering their world, they started coming to my world. Theological, salvation, apologetic, and "out-there" questions started coming my direction. This was walking with publicans and sinners.

3. *How did you legitimize your work? Who was necessary to come on board with your vision, and how did they buy in?*

We began with around 30 people who also wanted to make their Christianity practical to the community. We talked and dreamed for a few months and then officially started. We had struck a chord for "real and even messy gospel Christianity" not professional and programmed presentations. As the passion grew, we did not have a problem getting more to enjoy it. We have had some difficulties, of which I will talk later, but it has grown, not only numerically, but influentially from grace. When the heart of a Christian is touched by practical gospel grace, it only desires more of it. What is really cool is the new Christians that have not known any other type of church, and so they see it as normal. How much they have to learn!

Our legitimizing simply came from hearts of love for others without asking for anything in return. This was important to us. For example, I washed cookie sheets (and other things) at the coffee shop (Cool Beans). They began to offer me free things...

coffee, cookies, bakery, sandwiches…all of which I declined. I did not want any "payback" for my ministry. At times the owner demanded I try a cookie to get an opinion of its taste, but beyond that, I paid for everything.

4. *What price did you pay to create this ministry?*

Relationships. After four years of work and ministry, the "rubber hit the road." We had committed from the beginning that we would minister to anyone who comes through the door. So, past strippers, prostitutes, drug dealers, druggies, prisoners walked in along with strong and weak Christians, and they all received grace. All was good *until* the "lepers" came. Now we had a problem. Sex offenders are persona non grata to many people and even Christians. Let me quickly say that everyone agreed at the beginning to accept them specifically in our church. They would have to abide by a contract we wrote (having a shadow, limited movement, nothing with or near children). When a leper came, we had a test. Four years can change a way a person thinks. Some of the original 30 took issue with this, even though we had continually reiterated our desire to minister to the outcast, processed, and lepers of society. We lost one-third of the congregation, plus one-third of the financials. It was a price, but one that God granted us grace to pay.

Reputation. With the needy comes messy stuff. This last week we heard of a lady who used to come to our church [who was] gossiping and lying about us. She had been graciously confronted on her continuing sexual sins. She left. Now she is spewing out venom and junk, which will hurt our reputation. But we are not the first, nor will we be the last, to receive false accusations. Stay pure, love heartily, and hope deeply.

5) *What responses did you receive from those targeted by your newly begun micropolitan ministry?*

Gratitude. Wow! This morning I heard a convert say, "This individual loved me and cared for me when I was so messed up, no one could help. He came over, listened, and I knew he loved me honestly." That is worth it.

Commitment. By and large, those who have been rescued stay on the ship. But this is not always true. Some are on the take and go elsewhere when they can get more. But others? "Where no oxen are, the trough is clean; but much increase comes by the strength of an ox." Oxen are messy, and therefore, so is the trough. We have our fair share of oxen.

Joy, Happiness, Trust, Hope. It is all here. Don't get me wrong, we have troubles. But watching the whole church pray as one this morning is heart and soul warming and refining for grace.

6. *What specific lessons have you learned? What would you do differently?*

Love regardless. It is not ours to decide whether to love or hope. That is God's, and He has loved and given hope. I am to love the unlovely and unloving regardless.

Count your chickens before they hatch, or you won't see them. God brings the chickens and the eggs, so watch! He does according to His pleasure and we can trust in it. We teach our people to "Count and Care."

Accept pain as a sweet and sour friend. It is easy to fight against what God brings into the ministry, not knowing what it is teaching. Soon enough, you'll know lots more.

7. *What advice would you give to someone who was considering starting a new ministry in a micropolitan community?*

Be willing to wander for the kingdom of God.

Sprinfield, Ohio

Springfield, Ohio, has a population of approximately 60,000, Pastor Ted Rastatter, whose teammate is Pastor Dave Black, shared this:

1. *What were the specific considerations in your heart and mind as you began a new micropolitan ministry? (What was it that drove you to do this?)*

We spent time considering what we thought were missing from existing church philosophies in the area: what were untruths people believed about what church is and how to biblically redefine it; was there a church or ministry that could reach the type of people that we could reach?

2. *What initial steps did you take when you started your work (a new church or a need-meeting ministry)? Did you come as an insider, or as an outsider, to the community—and how did this factor into how you began?*

In forming a new church, I came as an insider to the community while the planting pastor came as an outsider. We canvassed by holding interest meetings with people we had already met. My being an insider factored in, because I could network very easily with people who have resources.

3. *How did you legitimize your work? Who was necessary to come on board with your vision, and how did they buy in?*

We learned it's necessary to have a plan in place for children before you start a service: children's workers, older believers, tech team, worship team, and people who would just commit to being at a function were all necessary. They bought in after specific conversations with staff and visiting the ministry.

4. *What price did you pay to create this ministry?*

I left a very cushy job as a worship pastor in a mega church. My salary dropped dramatically as I had to find other work while not being paid to help start the church. Monetarily, it was a large price to pay. I also led myself and my wife away from our home church where we grew up, so we paid with relationships. I have had to sacrifice excellence in my craft as a worship leader because having the perfect band is not possible when you are first starting.

5. *What specific lessons have you learned? What would you do differently?*

I would have a larger launch team with specific job descriptions for each person and wouldn't launch until all agreed to the expectations. I would also make sure that the starting pastor was fully supported by the church in order to not be bogged down with another job.

6. *What advice would you give to someone who was considering starting a new ministry in a micropolitan community?*

   I would research what a community really believes about Christ and redirect them to the Jesus in the Scripture.

Ashland, Ohio

Pastor Dan Allan, who is pastor of the mother church to a church plant in Ashland, Ohio, (population 21,000), shared this:

1. *What were the specific considerations in your heart and mind as you began a new micropolitan ministry? (What was it that drove you to do this?)*

   I kept looking at the people in our town who were *not* being reached. I couldn't help but notice that there was a large pocket of people (lower income, north/east end of town, county fair attenders) who were really not showing up in *any* church in town. So it seemed to me that we needed a different kind of church to reach a different kind of people.

2. *What initial steps did you take when you started your work (a new church or a need-meeting ministry)? Did you come as an insider, or as an outsider, to the community—and how did this factor into how you began?*

   My initial step was to pray. That was all I felt I could do. I knew I was not the guy to reach these people, but God put a heavy burden/compassion on my heart for them. I just pleaded for God to raise up someone to do something to reach him or her. And years later, God answered that prayer. The youth pastor and the youth group were the ones who began to penetrate this pocket of the community. They began some home Bible studies in the apartment complex where they lived…and a church was born!

3. *How did you legitimize your work? Who was necessary to come on board with your vision, and how did they buy in?*

   The work was legitimized by pointing to changed lives and saying, "This is the work of God!" The people with a heart for God and the unreached people in the town jumped on board. Many of these people had said that God had burdened them for the same people.

4. *What price did you pay to create this ministry?*

Time, energy, and serious dollars!

5. *What responses did you receive from those targeted by your newly-begun micropolitan ministry?*

There is an initial mistrust. The low income/under resourced really don't want to be another agency's project. We have really tried to point to what Christ is doing in them and through them. We also want them to know that they are doing something in the community that we (as the big, middle-class church) were unable to do.

6. *What specific lessons have you learned? What would you do differently?*

I've learned that God will raise up the people and resources to reach the people that He is drawing to Himself. Do keep a careful eye on remaining true to the Scriptures/gospel and being open to try *any* methods or styles.

7. *What advice would you give to someone who was considering starting a new ministry in a micropolitan community?*

Don't assume there are already enough churches in the town! Even in small towns there are *thousands* of people going to hell. Focus on them...pray for them...ask God to open doors for the gospel. Ask God for a vision for different churches for different people.

BosNYWash

Regarding the BosNYWash (Boston/New York/Washington) area of the Eastern Seaboard, Dr. Tim Boal, executive director of GO2 Ministries and pastoring in Telford, Pa., said this:

1. *What were the specific considerations in your heart and mind as you began a new micropolitan ministry? (What was it that drove you to do this?)*

The primary purpose of all of our church planting is God's glory and the need of people. We did not so much target a type of area, but found ourselves pursuing church plants where our trained leaders were feeling called.

2. *What initial steps did you take when you started your work (a new church or a need-meeting ministry)? Did you come as an insider, or as an outsider, to the community—and how did this factor into how you began?*

Our vision was to reach the BosNYWash region. We have allowed the leader to determine what model to use, based on his calling, passion, and demographic work.

3. *How did you legitimize your work? Who was necessary to come on board with your vision, and how did they buy in?*

Our elders, our congregation gave internal approval. Our church planters surveyed community leaders and local pastors for their buy-in to a new church in the community.

4. *What price did you pay to create this ministry?*

Our financial cost for the seven daughter churches have each cost a different amount. Our most expensive to date cost $71,000 and the least expensive cost $5,000. The human resource price was an additional 10-12 hours from two staff persons per week in ministry for 15 years engaging leadership training and vision-casting for church planting.

5. *What responses did you receive from those targeted by your newly-begun micropolitan ministry?*

Most were generally favorable, but probably because of the gifting of the church planter, rather than the fact that a new church was coming to town.

6. *What specific lessons have you learned? What would you do differently?*

We will go multi-site in the future rather than daughter church. Here is why. Multi-sites, which can become autonomous churches later, are similar to bringing a teenager to maturity and releasing him/her to the world as a young adult. Daughter church planting is too often like leaving a brand new baby on the doorstep to fend for itself. We will no longer do daughter church-planting in future plants for this reason.

7. *What advice would you give to someone who was considering starting a new ministry in a micropolitan community?*

   Make sure you understand the culture of the community as much as possible before beginning. Do a lot of ground work ahead of time, identifying the core cultural values of the micropolitan location. Also, have realistic expectations about how long it will take before an outsider is accepted and trusted, and if possible, use an insider to the community for better impact.

Ashland, Ohio

Pastor Nathan Wells, a church planter in Ashland, Ohio (21,000 in population), planted Eastgate Bible church as a daughter church to Pastor Dan Allan's mother church. Nathan shared:

1. *What were the specific considerations in your heart and mind as you began a new micropolitan ministry? (What was it that drove you to do this?)*

   As I saw the needs people have in needing Jesus in an under-resourced and under-reached area, I was deeply moved to reach those dear people.

2. *What initial steps did you take when you started your work (a new church or a need-meeting ministry)? Did you come as an insider, or as an outsider, to the community—and how did this factor into how you began?*

   In starting our new church, we came as outsiders. I came as a youth pastor and the youth group came to minister to the children in the area. The adult relationships came later.

3. *How did you legitimize your work? Who was necessary to come on board with your vision, and how did they buy in?*

   Ashland GBC, where I was the youth pastor at the time, needed to buy into the vision to reach the people in this section of town.

I have a great relationship with Pastor Dan Allan, which was key to this working. It was also imperative that my wife bought in on all this.

4. *What price did you pay to create this ministry?*

    This ministry brought a lot of uncertainty. Moving from youth pastor to church planter had its own risk—to my own ministry and to my family. The spiritual warfare intensified dramatically as we endeavored to plant this new church.

5. *What responses did you receive from those targeted by your newly-begun micropolitan ministry?*

    As we ministered to the people we targeted, they felt very cared for and Jesus' love became real to them. For many of them, His love became real for the first time.

6. *What specific lessons have you learned? What would you do differently?*

    I have learned that I must follow the Holy Spirit's leading in my life. I need to continue to discern His leading and follow it. What would I do differently? I would follow the Holy Spirit more aggressively.

7. *What advice would you give to someone who was considering starting a new ministry in a micropolitan community?*

    Do make sure that you follow the Holy Spirit in daily movements. Do expect great spiritual warfare and prepare for it and expect much time to pass before they trust you. Do, indeed, make sure that you get a coach!

Chapter 4

Where am I?

MICROPOLITAN AREAS

"Outside of a dog, a book is man's best friend.
Inside a dog, it's too dark to read."
Groucho Marx

"I'm desperately trying to figure out why
kamikaze pilots wore helmets."
Dave Edison

"Then Jesus said, "God's kingdom is like seed thrown on a field
by a man who then goes to bed and forgets about it."
(Mark 4:26-27a, Eugene Peterson, *The Message*)

It's not a formal demographic term, but I'll bet you know what I mean by the phrase "flyover territory." For decades now, popular media has recognized what those who live in less prominent areas instinctively realized. Large, glamorous communities, especially those on the east and west coasts of North America, are where the action is. The rest of the continent is a necessary nuisance, a place the beautiful people "fly over" on their way to more worthy destinations. You've heard about flyover territory, and it's possible you even live and minister there.

I grew up in flyover territory, in West Alexandria, Ohio, a town of 1,100 people. When I was a boy of seven or eight, more than anything I wanted to sign up for the Ronald McDonald Kids' Club, which would make me eligible for a lot of really cool stuff. The closest McDonald's was in Dayton, Ohio, 15 miles away. One day my mom and I were in Dayton, and we stopped at a McDonald's to get some food. Mom knew I wanted to sign up for the club. My constant nagging was wearing her down.

So there I was, filling out the card to enroll in the Kids' Club! I put down my name and birthday, but when I came to the address line I paused. I vividly remember thinking, "Would I get into the club if I put West Alexandria down as my town?" I stood there thinking about it and decided that I would not receive the information unless I put Dayton down in the address line—which I did. I never did receive the Kids' Club kit! I paid the price for undervaluing where I lived—and I never want to do that again.

It is easy to see flyover territory in this way. It's easy to undervalue where we live, especially when we live in a non-glamorous, not-well-known community. In ministry, it's easy to see flyover territory as a stepping stone toward something prominent. If that's our orientation, we could be in danger of missing a great opportunity to serve Christ and His Kingdom. And we don't want to do that.

Though a little boring or less stimulating, for the sake of clarity, let us look at some important demographic terms to help us work through the world in which GSE can work.

Population Terminology for the US and Canada

Let's take a quick look at necessary population terms for North America, both in the U.S. and Canada. The North American Mission Board of the Southern Baptist Convention has done much of the heavy lifting, making some helpful delineations.

U.S. Urban Area The U.S. Census defines urban areas as that which "have a population density of at least 1,000 people per square mile (386 per square kilometer) and surrounding census areas that have an overall density of at least 500 people per square mile (193 per square kilometer)."

Metropolitan These contain a core urban area of 50,000 or more population. According to the U.S. Census Bureau, there are 370 such metropolitan areas in the United States and Puerto Rico.

Consolidated Metropolitan Statistical Area (CMSA) The U.S. Government classifies these areas as consisting of two or more overlapping or interlocking urban communities (known as primary metropolitan statistical areas), with a total population of at least one million. CMSAs comprise the 25 largest metropolitan areas in the United States. The New York CMSA, for example, includes the primary metropolitan statistical areas of New York-Northern New Jersey-Long Island and New York-New Jersey-Connecticut.

Micropolitan Statistical Area We'll define this even more specifically in a moment, but for now understand that a micropolitan community contains an urban core of at least 10,000, but fewer than 50,000 residents. According to the U.S. Census Bureau, there are 565 micropolitan areas in the United States and Puerto Rico. Each metro or micro area consists of one or more counties and includes the counties containing the core urban area, as well as any adjacent counties that have a high degree of social and economic integration (as measured by commuting to work) with the urban core.

Small Town A small town is in its most simple form defined as a group of people that live in the same area in primary flow within a place of 2,500 to 9,999.

Rurban A term used to describe smaller towns that are rural geographically, but urban socially and are made up of educated, less traditional, white collar out-migrants from the urban areas attracted to the small-town lifestyle, a growing dissatisfaction with city living, less expensive housing, and better atmosphere for raising children.

Urban Sprawl The extensive expansion of the city outside of a city center and inner city characterized by low-density development, car-dependent transportation routes, and single-use zoning.

Gentrification The process of renewal, revitalization, and rebuilding of deteriorated urban property. This process also encompasses infill development of areas previously not developed initially.

Canada uses the following terms to describe population concentrations:

Central Business District (CBD) The commercial and often geographic heart of a city.

Central Municipality The central city or core city is the municipality in an urban area or metropolitan area that emerged historically as the most prominent in the urban area. Almost without exception, the name of the core city is also shared with the urban area.

Census Metropolitan Area A census metropolitan area (CMA) or a census agglomeration (CA) is formed by one or more adjacent municipalities centered on a large urban area (known as the urban core). A CMA must have a total population of at least 100,000 of which 50,000 or more must live in the urban core. A CA must have an urban core population of at least 10,000.

Census Subdivision (CSD) An area that is a municipality or an area that is deemed to be equivalent to a municipality for statistical reporting purposes (e.g. as an Indian reserve or an unorganized territory).

Urban Area An area that has more than 400 people per square kilometer and has more than 1,000 people. If two or more urban areas are within two kilometers of each other, they are merged into a single urban area.[1]

Micropolitan America

"Micropolitan" sounds like a contraction of "micro" and "metropolitan," which it is. It's a smaller version of a metropolitan area and has most of what is needed for modern living. A micropolitan area is defined by the U.S. Census Bureau as having at least one urban cluster of at least 10,000, but less than 50,000 population, plus adjacent territories that have high degrees of social and economic integration with the core—usually evidenced by commuting.[2]

The United States Office of Management and Budget (OMB) defines "metropolitan and micropolitan statistical areas according to published standards that are applied to Census Bureau data. The general concept of a metropolitan or micropolitan statistical area is that of a core area containing a substantial population nucleus, together with adjacent communities having a high degree of economic and social integration with that core."[3]

A "micropolitan statistical area" is a central city that has at least 10,000 people but not more than 49,999.[4] All other areas are considered metropolitan. As of June 2000 there are 362 metropolitan statistical areas and 560 micropolitan statistical areas in the US.[5] The largest city in each area is called the "principal city." Another source names 573 micropolitan areas in the US. These 573 micropolitan areas have 29.8 million residents and include 674 of the 3141 counties of the U.S.[6]

Micropolitan areas roared to the forefront (if a micropolitan anything could possibly roar!) around the year 2000. In the midst of a presidential election, where demographers and statisticians stay busy with their projections, something new was discovered. Our government recognized "changes outside cities and suburbs that have been brought on by development, migration and the economic shift from farming and manufacturing to service industries." These areas were too urban to be rural but too small to be metropolitan. The term "micropolitan" was born, places with rural sensibilities, but with enough power to stand on their own.

From church growth movements in the 1980s, church planting headed into the larger cities seeking the greater population centers. We must continue. But, in the midst of this movement, smaller towns and micropolitan areas started to be overlooked. In recent years the "rural rebound" has thrust many urbanites back to the smaller areas. Tom Nebel described this in *Big Dreams in Small Places*:

> Rural America lost 1.4 million people in the 1980s to urban and suburban areas, but more than 1.8 million people have reversed those numbers in the '90s and the first decade of the 21st century by moving to the smaller towns. [7]

Many reasons are put forth for this flight to non-urban communities including rediscovering personal roots, the ability to feel safe and secure, enjoyment of a true quality of life, reduction of stress, lower cost of living, finding favorable climate, enjoying health and wellness, and putting leisure back into life.

Implications for those with a call to spread the gospel in North America are significant. It means that besides targeting urban centers, the opportunities in small towns and micropolitan communities are many.

Jim Montgomery offers a helpful guideline resulting from his work in the Philippines and interaction with coworkers. Montgomery offers a DAWN (Disciple a Whole Nation) strategy. This strategy is simple and focuses on these matters:

> In summary, it is to mobilize the whole Body of Christ in whole nations and all nations to work most directly at completing the Great Commission by providing the incarnate presence of Christ in the form of local gatherings of believers within easy access of every person of every class, kind and condition. This is sometimes referred to as Saturation Church Planting (SCP), but it is much more than the mere multiplication of buildings and meeting places. It is the intent to see the life of Christ lived out in all its purity, power, truth and outreach in the midst of every neighborhood, village, tribal group or other identifiable entity in every nation and people group in the world.[8]

Montgomery sees the need for seven million new churches globally in order to take effective steps to fulfilling the Great Commission, giving us some guidelines to consider as we think through micropolitan work. His focus is global, but I find his metrics helpful to get us thinking about our micropolitan areas. He proposes these guidelines for us to consider so as to know when a region or area is "evangelized:"

1. There is an active, witnessing cell of believers in every village, town, urban neighborhood, and ethnic community in the country;

2. There is a church for every geographical group of 300 to 1,000 people;

3. There is a viable church within everyone's geographical and socio-cultural reach.[9]

What might that look like for us in the West with an eye toward church expansion work? Perhaps we can ask God for a spiritually healthy, reproducing, and witnessing group of believers in every micropolitan area. If we are using 10,000 as the lower size of a micropolitan city, we would have at least one active group of believers in each city of 10,000. There is definite thought that we have already achieved this today. In light of our current dilemma, this definition is not helpful.

Montgomery's focus on a group of witnessing, growing disciples reaching into each group of 300 to 1,000 people is helpful for us in this thinking. This would call for at least 10-33 such churches for just one city of 10,000 people. Within this reach of 10-33 churches, we would need to intentionally focus on the differing social/economic representations so as to be effective in a blanketed approach. But what about all the cities of 10,000 in the U.S. that do have at least 33 churches? Would it be fair to say that most cities this size in the U.S. have at least 33 churches? Perhaps yes. But what about 33 churches that are more solidly balanced between the modalic/sodalic need that Hugh Halter talks about?[10] Sodalic entities are those that desire to drive direct missional work in communities. Modalic entities are those that focus on our discipleship and perpetuation needs in the church family. What about 33 churches in each city of 10,000 that are active, witnessing groups developing robustly healthy disciples? I would think that such a movement would call for a church a day in each region upon which we are focusing.

Micropolitan Canada

As micropolitan is new in the U.S., it is even newer in Canada. Canada has not yet adopted the use of "micropolitan" in describing her areas and citizens. Canadian population realities draw attention to the vast opportunities here. Currently, of the 184 largest cities in Canada, 132 are between 10,000 and 50,000 in population. In other words, there are 132 micropolitan communities in Canada—and about one-third of all Canadians live in them. According to the Annual Demographic Statistics of Canada (year 2005), more than 65 percent of Canadians or 21,030,100 people resided in census metropolitan areas (CMAs). Somewhat more than half of these people lived in the three largest CMAs: Toronto (5,304,100), Montréal (3,635,700) and Vancouver (2,208,300).[11] So, about half of those 65 percent, or about one-third of the Canadian population, lives in micropolitan communities.

What does this mean? It means that in the U.S. and Canada there are approximately 700 micropolitan areas, many of which are underserviced by the gospel. And if what is true for small towns is true for micropolitan areas, these are some of the "easiest" places to plant churches and do ministry. Market forces are minimized, "good" looks "great," and when something positive happens, the word spreads like wildfire. The opportunities are almost unbelievable.

How Do You Know You're in Flyover Territory?

There are a number of ways to tell.

You are in a "stand alone" community:

Smaller communities often have glass bubbles over them. What do I mean? They have their own cultural distinctive, even though they may be close to a larger metropolitan center. Mount Sterling is 10 miles south of Columbus, Ohio. When I am in Mount Sterling, I know that I am no longer in Columbus. Columbus' long tentacles do not reach down entirely into Mount Sterling. The bubble is like a force-field, which preserves its own cultural integrity. If properly understood, those who minister in such places can leverage these distinctions for good.

We planted in a small town and began the new church in a home. We then moved to the local community center. The community center welcomed us with open arms to use the facility without charge. To this day (now two-plus years later) they still are willing to allow us to use the space—without charge. (Shhhh!)

Why? As you enter this community center, you read its purpose statement. As you move down the nicely framed 8½ x 11 sheet of paper, you read how this community center is established for helping the residents in their spiritual pursuits! I'm not sure I would read a purpose statement like that in a large community. And the board of directors of the community center believed the statement. At their monthly meeting, when our request was presented, they responded quickly and with a resounding "yes." We offered to pay. They said no; use it for free.

This is an example of the different kind of "bubble" that exists in micropolitan areas.

Greater familiarity:

The interaction that is forced by a smaller population base creates a sense of greater familiarity. One way I know I am in a micropolitan area is when I am driving my car and people walking on the street wave at me. They do not know me, but they wave anyway. My home for 19 years was in the suburbs of Columbus, Ohio. So, I drove there often—every day. No one waved to me where I lived, even when I waved at him or her first!

So, the difference I experienced was great. When I drove around the smaller towns, the open willingness to wave to begin an initial acknowledgement was amazing. I have come to expect and enjoy that.

Another example of familiarity to me is the first time I drove my pickup truck to this small town. I knew I was in a micropolitan area when I pulled into town and parked near a local restaurant and my truck was just one of an entire row of pickup trucks. It had an interesting impact on me.

The impact it had on me was this: "I am at home here. I do not know anyone, really, but I feel at home." I cannot express how important that feeling was as we moved on in establishing a ministry in that town.

The individual does matter:

The individual matters everywhere. But the more faces there are in a particular place, the more they all blend together. This is the challenge of a metropolitan ministry—giving individuality to a mass of people that can all look the same, though they are all screaming out their individuality.

In flyover territory the individual is more noticeable.

Carolyn Shotsky, life-long citizen of a micropolitan town, says, "[The] lifestyle is slower. There is not as much temptation to buy things we don't really need anyhow. I have the previous four generations of ancestors buried within 20 miles of me, and they are in the local history books…the individual matters."

Along this line of thinking, we need to note that these smaller micropolitan communities generally do not respond as well to mass communication efforts. The reasons for this are at least two-fold: 1) It is hard to get up to a critical mass of at least 10,000 pieces to distribute to begin having measurable results; and 2) since the individual matters to this level, effective individual contact works well at this level.

Local church connectivity:

Micropolitan areas tend to have differing church connections. This idea is well reflected by John and Sheri J., who say, "We need to be aware that the various congregations in the community are connected. We can accomplish more by working together, rather than just focusing on what our local church is doing. We affect each other more in a small community."

Carolyn adds, "In my opinion…the denominations of Christian churches blend together. They all have their own services and little 'societies,' but a lot of projects take all of them working together to make it happen. I have no doubt that God smiles on those days!

Don't miss the opportunity:

I saw a few episodes of the TV show *Lost*. It has an intriguing concept. There is a very secret place on that island. Everyone can get off the island, but they do not. There is something holding them there. They call the show *Lost* for good reason.

Jesus has secrets about where He places people. We just have to figure out those "secrets" and use them to reach the people Jesus has placed there. We often call this "exegeting our community." Whether I am in a big or small city or even a rural location with just a few people, I know Jesus loves them and shed His blood to provide salvation to them, touching their lives now and forever. I hope to share some of the "secrets" of reaching flyover territory in Jesus' name.

These "secrets" are what Jesus has told us to do: "Go therefore and make disciples of all the nations, baptizing them in the name of the Father and the Son and the Holy Spirit, teaching them to observe all that I commanded you; and lo, I am with you always, even to the end of the age." (Matthew 28:19-20). The "secret" part of this Great Commission is how we take Jesus' command and apply it to the various places.

Have you ever been lost? There is lost and then there is LOST. When I am lost, I often find my way quickly. I am a pastor and visit many people. I can find just about anybody! But when I am LOST, it gets scary. I am LOST when I begin to get scared because I do not recognize any streets or landmarks. But I am sure I am not alone.

My wife and I recently took a trip from Columbus, Ohio, to Atlanta, Georgia. As we were heading down Rt. 75, our Garmin told us to get off on Rt. 68 in Tennessee. Big mistake. We were not lost. The Garmin knew exactly where we were. But we did not want to be here! Rt. 68 in southern Tennessee and northern Georgia is not a straight road!

The ease of driving the four-to-eight lane wide, super highway Rt. 75 and the difficulty of driving the narrow, curvy, hilly, tree-lined Rt. 68 was a contrast. I knew where I was, but I did not want to be there.

In micropolitan ministry, we can be in a similar situation. We're not really lost, but not sure we want to be there.

Postmodern hunger for relationship is clearly expressed:

Hunger for authentic and real relationships that exist in our current culture shows itself in every living condition and situation. Rural and small town relationship expressions do differ from metropolitan, suburban, and micropolitan environments.

Micropolitan expressions of relationship are often subjectively viewed as "Mayberry" type thinking. Small towns are definitely Mayberry-like relational expressions; micropolitan cities have this flavor in definite pockets.

Culture is hard to define. Merriam Webster defines culture: "the set of values, conventions, or social practices associated with a particular field, activity, or societal characteristic; and the customary beliefs, social forms, and material traits of a racial, religious, or social group; also: the characteristic features of everyday existence (as diversions or a way of life) shared by people in a place or time."

With this as a beginning point, micropolitan communities show themselves differently from urban centers and small town areas.

Notes

[1]North American Mission Board, "Defining the North American Urban Context," brochure, December 2, 2008

[2]Metropolitan Statistical Areas, Micropolitan Statistical Areas, Combined Statistical Areas, New England City and Town Areas, and Combined New England City and Town Areas – 2003, p. 2

[3]U.S. Census Bureau, "About Metropolitan and Micropolitan Statistical Areas," http://census.gov/population/www/estimates/about-metro.html (accessed 1/25/2005); see also http://geography.about.com/cs/largecities/a/metromicro.htm (accessed 1/25/2005)

[4]El Nasser, "For Political Trends, Think Micropolitan;" also census.gov

[5]U.S. Census Bureau, "About Metropolitan and Micropolitan Statistical Areas," http://census.gov/population/www/estimates/about-metro.html (accessed 1/25/2005)

[6]El Nasser, "For Political Trends, Think Micropolitan."

[7]Tom Nebel, *Big Dreams in Small Places,* 13.

[8]Steele, "A Case Study in Cooperative Evangelism," 3.

[9]Montgomery, *DAWN 2000*, 49

[10]Halter and Smay, 2010, 131 ff.

[11]*Statistics Canada,* "Annual Demographic Statistics 2005, Catalogue no. 91-213-XIB," 32.

SECTION 2

ADVANTAGES AND IMPACT OF GSE

Chapter 5
ADVANTAGES TODAY

"The way to get started is to quit talking and begin doing . . ."
Walt Disney

"Stop worrying—nobody gets out of this world alive."
Clive James

"I didn't skimp or trim in any way. Every truth and encouragement
that could have made a difference to you, you got."
Paul - Acts 20:20 (Eugene Peterson, *The Message*)

Today is a day of unprecedented opportunity. When it comes to starting new churches, it makes sense to capitalize on ways to see the greatest amount of fruit. Some denominations need victories in church planting. Some denominations have neglected church planting for so long that they leave no systems necessary to do church planting.

Economic realities force us to take another look at how church planting occurs. Some of our denominations can no longer afford to pour thousands of dollars into a single church plant. We need to explore other ways to see the fruit we desire.

Gimli the Dwarf, in *Lord of the Rings*, was one who recognized opportunity when he saw it. In *The Return of the King*, as the battle was raging on the Plain of Pellinor outside the gates of Minas Tirith, he saw opportunity. Sauron had launched his last battle to destroy the realm of man. The darkness of Mount Doom's realm and the land of Mordor had been extended so the orcs, who could not do well in light, could function in the extended battle. The horsemen from Gondor had arrived and made their impact, but the enemies' numbers were too large.

Then the boats arrived at the harbor. The orc in charge wanted the dark-sided humans on board the boats to come off and join in the battle. Aragorn jumped off, Legolas and Gimli jumped off, then the realm of the dead who were fulfilling their oath to Aragorn's great-grandfather jumped off.

As Gimli and Legolas walked toward the battle, Gimli said, "There are plenty of them for both us, may the best dwarf win!" Legolas and Gimli had this issue throughout the movie series regarding which one of them would kill the most orcs. On the plains of Pellinor, Gimli did not see an overwhelming number of enemies. He saw plenty of opportunity!

We live in a day of opportunity, if we have our eyes focused to see as Jesus would see.

In Matthew 9:35-39, Matthew tells us: "Jesus was going through all the cities and villages, teaching in their synagogues and proclaiming the gospel of the kingdom, and healing every kind of disease and every kind of sickness. Seeing the people, He felt compassion for them, because they were distressed and dispirited like sheep without a shepherd. Then He said to His disciples, 'The harvest is plentiful, but the workers are few. Therefore beseech the Lord of the harvest to send out workers into His harvest (NASB).'"

Micropolitan Opportunities Focused in Church Development Phases

Also, in John 20:21, John tells us: "So Jesus said to them again, 'Peace *be* with you; as the Father has sent Me, I also send you (NASB).'"

"People flight" to the city is no longer the growing attraction. Some city dwellers have left the city for the smaller communities. Ex-urban is the name for this phenomenon. Someone is exurban when he/she lives in a region or settlement that lies outside a city (usually beyond its suburbs) and that often is inhabited chiefly by well-to-do families.[1] Micropolitan church planting has advantages. Church planting using other, more cost effective models is advantageous. There are advantages in each of the church formation phases.

Advantages in Micropolitan Church Planting Phases

All church planting is difficult, but micropolitan communities boast certain advantages that assist in the process. To review from a previous chapter, micropolitan communities bring to the "advantages table" the following:

You are in "stand alone" territory.

People have greater familiarity with one another.

Individual values are expressed in the community.

Local churches can have high connectivity.

Opportunities that we do not want to miss present themselves.

Postmodern hunger for relationship is clearly expressed.

Micropolitan Ministry Advantages Expressed in Birthing Phases

Church birthing needs are obvious everywhere in America. As we strive to plant more and more churches, a model is needed to evaluate where a church exists in the process. The more common model used to evaluate or describe the church-planting process is a biotic model. In exploring the biotic forms, we can focus on birthing churches in micropolitan areas. A biotic model is helpful because it shows the basics of church planting in understandable terms and forms. These phases are helpful when discussing the development of new churches.

Birthing Phase 1: Conception—Making Babies Is Fun!

Logan and Ogne explain the phases of the biotic model of church planting. The first is the conception phase. This phase deals with all the tasks that must be accomplished before actually beginning the process of planting the new church.[2] Matters developed in this phase include call confirmation in the heart of the planter, initial assessment of the planter, and completion of the vision documents prepared by the planter. This conception phase is foundational, perhaps even most important. What happens in the heart of the church planter is critical. When the church planters "see" the new church

Jesus has birthed in their hearts, they can lead others to see that picture in their heart fulfilled!

This phase is enjoyable because there are no obstacles except our own hearts. Those involved at this early level are already on board with what church planting is all about. They are all cheerleaders for the same thing—the conception of a new church in a planter's heart!

When I am coaching a church planter and have the privilege to be connected at this early phase, it is actual "party time" when we are able to recognize when this conception phase has occurred. A friend of mine, Nathan, has proven to be a very effective church planter. His passion for telling people about Jesus is intense, and his desire for new churches is powerful. One of his desires is to take control of a local bar in his part of God's Kingdom and plant a church in it!

On a recent occasion, Nathan and I were working through a current potential church planting project. It soon became evident that Jesus had birthed a church in his heart in the east side of this Midwest city—Mansfield, Ohio (population 49,000). As we realized how profound Nathan's remarks were, we stopped and recommended a party! It was time to celebrate! Jesus had just formed a new church in Ohio—though it had not moved beyond Nathan's heart. But Jesus had done His conception phase work in Nathan's heart. Nothing moves ahead without someone "seeing" it!

Birthing Phase 2: Prenatal—Now We Can Become Uncomfortable!

The second phase is called the prenatal phase,[3] which has key considerations in the planting process. More church plant failures can be traced to this phase than any other.[4] This phase involves the various approaches to core group gathering. A core group is key to any church plant. The church planter is challenged on all fronts in forming this all-important core group.

In the VisionOhio Operations Center, we use a metric phrase to help us come to grips with measuring core group activity: "Five families to come alive (as a church) and 25 to thrive (go public with the new church)."[5] With a Gatherer/Shepherd/ Elder (GSE) process, we tone it down to "three families to come alive (as a church) and 12 to thrive (go public with the new church)."

Prenatal goals like these help us keep a common measuring stick in the conversation. A church can launch or go public with fewer than 25 families or 12 families. We just know that the larger the core group at launch time, the better the outcome.

Birthing Phase 3: Birth—Excitement and Pain!

The third phase is the birth phase.[6] This phase shows that the prenatal phase has worked. This phase implements systems that serve the church for a long time. These systems are critical for long-term development. The three key systems necessary for all new church plants are: 1) some form of a shepherding system/pastor care provision; 2) some form of child care system; 3) some form of public worship system. Each of these systems forms key thoughts and sets the direction for the new church.

Planters can have varying levels of meltdown in this phase. We can talk about a hard launch or soft launch. A hard launch is when many resources go into "going public" after a lot of work in the conception phase. A soft launch is when fewer resources go into the public notification that there is a new church. Either way, the public launch, in whatever form it takes, is when we tell the community in which the new church resides that we are here.

Much is involved with giving birth. When my wife gave birth to both our children, 22 months apart, we had a similar pathway. The bag was packed for the hospital stay; we had kid coverage at home for the birth of the second child; insurance (if we had it) was all in order; the doctor was ready, and so on.

Birthing a new church is similar. There are many preparations for the birth, and after the birth, and when the child is born, it is never the same. Everything changes. So there are many forces that impact us as the new church experiences a public birth.

Birthing Phase 4: Reproduction—More Fun!

The fourth phase is the reproduction phase.[7] This is the phase in which the new church gives birth to her first daughter church. This step is a hard one. If a new church does not plant in the first five years, it is not likely that it will.

There are always exceptions. Southwest Grace in Grove City, Ohio, was 20 years old when she birthed her first church. Southwest Grace began in 1977 and her first daughter church was planted in 1997. She then worked toward five more birthings in the next 12 years. Eastgate Bible (Ashland, Ohio) is a new church plant that is three years old. It is planting a new church with key congregational involvement in another community in year three.

Advantages

Instead of placing a founding pastor in a town or city from the first day, the GSE process focuses on using a gathering and shepherding team to form a core group, then seeking the Lord of the harvest for an elder to lead the group to greater formation. The gatherer's job is to make contacts and give invitations to people who live in the town. The shepherd on the field is to work in combination with the gatherer to found the church. As these two work in tandem, the group grows and is ready for a biblically qualified elder/pastor to be placed on the field.

This GSE process takes advantage of the micropolitan advantages listed above. It uses these advantages well:

- You are in stand-alone territory. The GSE connects well to areas in which differing culture is expressed because at least the gatherer and elder understand that particular culture because they are part of it. When a new or differing culture expresses itself, that is a great place to begin a new church.

- People have greater familiarity with one another. The gathering work in the GSE is profoundly useful in making relational connections in an area where people are familiar with one another. There are some cultural expressions where fences are walls—tall walls. Micropolitan areas tend to allow fences to be just that.

- Individual values are expressed in the community. Gatherers are, by nature, men and women who live by their values. They are people who like to hear the values of others. When there are opportunities to connect with other people's values, the essence of gathering is in the micropolitan advantage area.

- Local churches can have high connectivity. The GSE process is best done with local church connection. The more "blessing" that occurs in a GSE process, the better this process will go.

- Opportunities present themselves that we do not want to miss. Momentum is an important piece of church planting. As a gatherer picks up steam in his inviting work and gathering process, the opportunities that present themselves are ones we need to fully grasp.

- Postmodern hunger for relationship is clearly expressed. The hunger for relationship is perhaps the most powerful piece presenting itself in the list of advantages the micropolitan area offers. As a gatherer does his work, the fruit and momentum that results is clear.

- Clearly distinctive culture differs from larger metropolitan cultures. Gatherers have the real possibility, through effective coaching and oversight, of becoming specific cultural experts in their work. They may not understand how they are able to do this well, but the fact is that their fruit can express itself most clearly in the smaller, distinct cultural areas.

Connection in the GSE Process

The GSE micropolitan process is *connected, missional, and has non-Sunday beginning points.* Connected means this new church has a connection with an established church that is preferably nearby, though not necessarily close. To be "connected" covers more than money, since this process does not require much (or any) money to begin. More important are the prayer and coaching support. The term "mother church" is used in those situations in which financial resources are involved. For situations in which financial resources are not involved, we are using the term "connected."

Sterling Grace was launched from Southwest Grace. Sterling Grace was birthed in a smaller micropolitan community 15 miles south of Grove City, Ohio, in a town called Mount Sterling. The connection piece was critical. Because of the proximity of the two churches, key aid and "not feeling alone" was averted.

Missional Aspects (Missionary Aspects) of the GSE Process

The second characteristic of our GSE process is missional. Stetzer defines missional this way: "Plant a church that's part of the culture you're seeking to reach."[8] For a church to be "part of the culture you are seeking to reach" is an important thought. We can move toward using the term missional as we take advantage of this culture. This missional component is what must drive the diversity of church methodologies or styles of plants. Each church plant must have the presentation of the Gospel of Jesus Christ, but focus on the cultural expression unique to reaching a particular segment of the population is key.

Non-Sunday Beginning Points of the GSE Process

The third characteristic, non-Sunday beginning points, is important for at least two reasons. First, the issue of connection is more effective when the new church does not meet at the same time as the church with who they are in connection. This can allow joint participation between a family at the connecting church and the church plant. When we began Sterling Grace, I was pastoring at Southwest Grace and preaching on Sunday mornings. We began on Thursday nights and then moved to Sunday nights. My involvement was possible because of this non-Sunday morning beginning.

Another reason for the non-Sunday morning starting point is that it allows for significant storytelling and thus prayer support between the established church and the GSE effort. As stories are told about what God is doing in the GSE, the established church has the opportunity to have her own engines revved and excitement heightened.

Micropolitan communities tend to have a preconception of Sunday morning church. Those in the community may receive an alternative option as interesting or refreshing. This alternative cuts both ways. A non-Sunday morning beginning can be a point of real interest among people in the community. The community may need a Sunday morning service at some time; for some this is key. Each community can be different, so as the team "exegetes" the community, it can find out what is the best way to get this done.

Postmodern Opportunities

In addition to advantages in micropolitan church planting, there are advantages today because of postmodernism. Postmodernism is often a bad word. Postmodernism does have positive impact on church planting. For the church, our modern culture is often looked down upon in a very disparaging way. Our present postmodern culture is often blamed for "losing my church!" Many long-standing church goers are experiencing drastic shifts in what has always been "their church." These changes are not well received, because who does enjoy change? No one!

Our current postmodern culture is many things, but it is a time of great opportunity!

Postmodernism's Positive Impact upon Church Planting in North America

When I graduated from seminary in 1986, I was loaded for theological bear and ready to get to work. I thought, as did most who were formally trained as I was, that if I can only explain "it" to them, they will come! Wrong! I was well prepared and do not regret the training at all. My training allowed me to move into other areas of ministry.

As I have moved through 25 years of vocational ministry, the changes have been great. But connecting to the changes has been the key area of my focus. Postmodernism's changes have been great. Church change has been great, even in my own denomination.

One great advantage I have is something my dad taught me. He always wanted me to be open to opportunities that exist. I hated raking leaves. I grew up in a small town of 1,100 people. Large houses with half-acre lots were the norm. Now this half-acre lot had many big trees on it, large maple trees mostly. I remember at least 12 big maple trees. These trees lost their leaves at the same time. Guess who got to rake the leaves to the curb so they could be hauled away? Me. In my recollection, my brother never had to rake leaves. (Now he may disagree with that statement.)

Why all this? I dreaded it and always saw it as a herculean task. I only saw it one way—my way. And my way was only concerned about me and how much work I had to do before I got to what I really liked, like basketball or running. Each year the task fell to me and each year I hated it. To this day, I dread (though not hate) raking leaves. I even have a device that blows the leaves, but I still dread it, even with new tools! The new tools have helped me move from hating raking leaves to now, simply dreading it.

New tools make it easier. Postmodernism is a new tool with a great advantage to us. I do not need to "hate" the changes that have occurred over time, though I can easily justify "hating" postmodernism's effect on the church. I can embrace postmodernism differently and see how I can use it to Jesus' advantage.

A few years ago, I had a vivid experience while sitting in my office at the church I pastored for 19 years. Ministry was humming along and going pretty well. We were seeing people come to faith, share their faith, grow in their faith, and reproduce themselves in others. But one day I was sitting in my office looking out the window at the parking lot and adjacent wooded lot. From books I was reading and from listening to people, I knew we were in the venue of change. The beginning of the end hit me at that time. It finally began to sink deep into my heart that "things" would never be the same at my church, and my ministry would never be the same.

I think I had enough insight to realize that the way I had been "doing" ministry would never be the same! I would not be able to use the same "tricks of the trade" I had used before and get the same positive results. That day was a hard day. My life changed dramatically that day. Those thoughts only scratched the surface of how the changes would affect me. It is actually good I did not know how drastic the postmodern change would be on me.

Postmodernism is more than a catchword. It is a mindset with powerful implications in all we do for Jesus Christ. It is not a bad word in church planting circles. As a matter of fact, postmodernism brings powerful allies that assist in church planting. We will look at several examples.

But first, there is something we need to explore. Postmodernism is a term first coined by Frederico de Onis in 1930s. But the term did not achieve prominence until it was used to describe art and literature in the 1960s and architecture in the 1970s. Then in the 1980s it came to be the favorite word describing what our current culture is doing.[9] In short summary, the greatest benefit postmodernism has brought to us is the need or opportunity to think about our western culture from the missionary perspective and to engage ministry from this aspect.

Sodalic Entities: Those Other Kind of People

Sodalic, also called centrifugal, individuals are people of great passion. They desire to go where we have not gone before. Their passion comes from their connection with Jesus Christ and their understanding of the mission He has given uniquely to them. Sodalic thinking is valued in a postmodern culture. Passion expressed through a sodalic individual works well because of the intense questioning and critiquing of our world done by the current culture. These people are the ones who ask many penetrating questions. They see things differently. They do so because they carry such a high passion for their Lord.

A sodalic or centrifugal person is (most likely) anyone who has had the conception phase of the biotic church birthing model happen in his or her heart! When Jesus births a new church in the heart of one of His planters, passion is extreme! Careful insight into this concept allows us to see the first phase of birthing new churches. The conception phase is when Jesus gives birth to His new church in this person's heart. Sodalic people are those who live in light of these realities.

Those who are sodalic are perhaps better able to serve as missionaries because they think differently about mission. Stetzer clarifies that missiological thinking, "requires an understanding of the church's biblical identity, its loss of that identity, and its need to rediscover an indigenous expression of that identity in each culture."[10]

Cultural Rhythms: Grasping the "Every Day"

In Regele's book *The Death of the Church,* he shares two key characteristics of postmodern thought that assist us in church planting: 1) generational types, and 2) the crisis movement toward a more "do" based culture (after having moved from an "experience" based culture).[11]

Understanding generational types is important to forming the target group of a new church.[12] Using this type of information and information gathering—as Regele has—can assist us as we work through the process of core gathering and launch team formation.[13]

Meanwhile, an outer-directed cultural rhythm that values "doing" what Jesus wants is truly an advantage for church planting. Though this value can lead to institution building, church planting is the necessary precursor. In America, there will not be greater growth or building of institutions without planting more churches.

Metanarratives: First of the Postmodern "Unholy Trinity." Not Accepting the Old Answers

Postmodernism is often reduced to three key thoughts or fixtures of understanding. The first one for us is this: post moderns reject any metanarrative. A metanarrative is any large based story that centers man as a solution to some cultural problem. We are currently rejecting modern metanarratives such as evolution and Communism, but we are open to a story like Christianity. In the church-planting context, the early years are well formed by many individual conversations and the ability to know one another quite closely. My experience shows that postmodern individuals desire such a focus.

The church planter-gatherers can excel in their work of telling the story of Jesus. They no longer need to equip themselves with apologetic arguments that were important to modern individuals in order to share the gospel with them. Though many modern thinkers still walk the planet and need the story of Jesus, they too are influenced by the postmodern turn, which quiets the demand for rational apologetics. Presuppositional apologetics remain as powerful tools at our disposal.[14]

It is a relief that I no longer need to "ask permission" before I talk about Jesus with a person. Metanarrative rejection infuses this opportunity, so that as I build a relationship with a person, we can talk about anything—even Jesus Christ— without a long, nerve-racking soliloquy setting up the opportunity.

President Lyndon Johnson said that we would see poverty solved or wiped out by the 1980s. That did not happen. I remember in middle school/jr. high that I was told that by the time I would be in the workplace, there would be so much help from technology that I would work a three-day work week. I missed something somewhere! These two metanarrative examples show one blessing postmodernism has given to us.

Interpretation: Second Part of the Postmodern "Unholy Trinity." What truth means.

Post moderns have challenged our concept of absolute truth. The Scriptures are absolute truth. We live in a cultural day that says truth is how I see it, not how you see it. One side benefit of this alarming reality is how open people are to listening. There seemed to be a day when, if you could get a chance to share Jesus Christ with someone, there was a lot of fruit. Today there may be more opportunities to talk about Jesus, but perhaps less fruit because of this tendency. But this works fine. If I find it easier to talk about Jesus, then a huge hurdle has been removed in my heart for sharing Jesus Christ.

Hence, the church planter-gatherer does not have to argue with post moderns to tell the story of Jesus.[15] He or she can be assured of some form of listening ears.[16] This is a valuable asset in church planting because the need to get the story out and form the core group is critical to the process of church planting. Another postmodern asset in church planting is the openness to *sola scriptura* and the Holy Spirit's role in the process.[17] The sodalic individual with great passion to form a new church has great assets on his/her side!

Power is knowledge: Third member of Post modern's "Unholy Trinity." What I Know

Post moderns flock to the concept that power is knowledge. Facts are more than facts in this day. While I was growing up, I could study and know the facts of something and it would just mean I studied that day. Often it did little to empower me. Today, this is different. The same set of facts brings a new empowerment to the individual. Godin's book *Tribes* illustrates well this idea when he repeatedly challenges us to lead. No matter who you are, you are a leader somewhere with someone to lead. This concept seems to glean some of its power from this postmodern concept.

The concept that power is knowledge also helps the planter as he tells the story and works to "do" the truth. The gatherer can be encouraged by this new turn. Smith speaks of the advantage spiritual disciplines can play in light of this particular cultural turn.[18] A church planter/gatherer has this in his arsenal of tools as the work continues in the core gathering process.

Bounded Set/Centered Set: Legalism or Freedom

Many churches bred from modernism apply a bounded set approach to formational spiritual life in their church families. In a bound set, rules and regulations characterize the journey. This can easily be understood as legalism. In this pattern of thinking, one must fit into a group's way of life, their bounded set, before belonging to it. If I want to belong to this particular group or church then I have to conform to what they want me to be. If I do not conform, then I do not feel welcome because I am not. The communication device is not the tongue. It is the non tangibles of relationships within a defined group.

The centered set and its derivative, the formational set, are characterized by movement toward the cross. Movement toward Jesus is acceptable and preferred.[19] Though this choice has always been available to a church family, postmodernism causes us to lean toward this formational set. The advantage to this way of posturing ourselves is that it makes us open to any sojourner who is on the same journey as we are. We are obviously at different places on the journey, but that is OK. We are going the same direction. The other person does not have to conform to me and my behavioral (or supposed behavioral) habits. We can truly be together on a journey toward Jesus.

Advocacy – Taking Action

Regele is right when he says, "*The primary unit of mission as we move into the 21ˢᵗ century must be, indeed will be, the local congregation.*"[20] The postmodern turn has brought us great opportunity. We need to target and exegete the people and communities we desire to plant with new churches. We also need to re-exegete the communities in which churches currently exist, so they will have a more effective impact! We must continue to reproduce local congregations equipped for ministry.

Too many churches and too many pastors are lost to ministry; 1,500 pastors per month leave the ministry.[21] Most of these ministers do not return to vocational ministry. The key is working harder at fixing this problem and adapting our strategies to better touch the lives and hearts of pastors, their families, and the church. Advocacy is important not only for the planter and his family, but also for those targeted. How can we best advocate for someone who needs the gospel? As we answer this question, we draw closer to being the advocates we need to be for these dear folks who need Jesus.

Missional Focus on Small Things: Can I Possibly Be Excited About Small Beginnings?

Zechariah 4:10 says, "For who has despised the day of small things? But these seven will be glad when they see the plumb line in the hand of Zerubbabel – these are the eyes of the Lord which range to and fro through the earth (NASB)." The postmodern turn values the day of the small things of which Zechariah speaks.[22] Wright describes the process: focus on the right stuff, hunger for God, build community, and see beauty.[23] While mission statements are important, the recognition that "small things" are also important is exciting.

Gospel Focus on Our Present Circumstances

The message of the gospel must also be addressed to a post-secular theology. Jesus was persistent in explaining how the gospel changes people's lives in the present (Mark 10: 28ff; Luke 10:25-29; 10:17-20; 18:18-30 to name a few). Much of the modern focus has been on the future: what do the future and heaven hold for me? The need to focus on Jesus' desire to impact the present is important, especially in light of Descartes' revelation of the self.[24] It is critical not only to "tell the story of Jesus" but also to "tell the story of Jesus and how He impacts my now."[25]

A missional focus keeps its eschatology in mind. Modernism's eschatology was progress; postmodernism's eschatology is crisis.[26] This crisis, often fear-based thinking and living, gives us a missional advantage in that it breeds a marginalized mindset. The Scriptures were written both to and from a marginalized context. Neither the writers nor the readers of the Bible were in control of anything in their culture. Hence, hope becomes a foundational, almost apocalyptic concept. We can use hope to center our message.

The church plant environment is one of great ease and diversity. Simple methods like welcoming, using Scripture, and modeling are well-suited to a church plant. Smith affirms these concepts as postmodern positives.[27] For the church planter to welcome someone who is without Christ while not affirming his/her sin is the essence of a church plant.[28] For a church plant to use Scripture more than an established church is easy. The small nature of church plants readily assists modeling or living out the story more than the established church.

Church planter-gatherers can take advantage of the postmodern turn. Established churches can take advantage of these positives as well. The Great Commission directs all who desire to work, and God continues to give clear advantages in the process of this work. Though the challenges are great, so too are the blessings and advantages we have in our arsenal. May God receive the glory as work in this current age continues and as He plants many new churches in Ohio. One exceptionally key aspect of church planting is the issue of expectations. Investing in a conversation on expectations is key.

Notes

[1]Webster's II New Riverside University Dictionary, (Boston: Riverside Pub. Co., 1984, s.vv. "exurb, exurbanite"

[2]Logan and Ogne, *Churches Planting Churches*, 4-6.

[3]Ibid, 4-7

[4]Terry Hofecker, classroom discussion, 2006.

[5]Vision Ohio, staff discussions, 2007

[6]Logan and Ogne 1995, 4-7.

[7]Ibid 4-5.

[8]Stetzer, *Planting Missional Churches*, 1.

[9]Gibbs, *Church Next,* 2000, 23.

[10]Stetzer, *Planting Missional Churches*, 27, see also 124.

[11]Regele, *Death of the Church,* 32ff, 40-42 and 112.

[12]Terry Hofecker, classroom discussion, 2007.

[13]Searcy and Thomas, *Launch: Starting a New Church from Scratch,* 143.

[14]Smith, *Who is Afraid of Postmodernism,* 50.

[15]Ibid, 58

[16]Ibid, 55

[17]Ibid, 55ff

[18]Ibid, 107

[19]*Pastors of Excellence*, 13

[20] *Death of the Church*, 219; emphasis Regele

[21]*Leaders that Last*, 10

[22]Bauckham, *Bible and Mission: Christian Witness in a Postmodern World*, 28 focuses here on the idea of God singling out Abraham

[23]Wright, *Simply Christian: Why Christianity Makes Sense*, 3-54

[24]Penner, *Christianity and the Postmodern Turn*, 75.

[25]Bauckham, *Bible and Mission*, 10.

[26]Allan Bevere, classroom discussion, 2007.

[27]Smith, *Who's Afraid of Postmodernism*, 76ff.

[28]Allan Bevere, classroom discussion, 2007.

Chapter 6

REGIONAL STRATEGIES: ONE A DAY

*"The formulation of a problem is often more essential
than its solution, which may be merely a matter of
mathematical or experimental skill."*
Albert Einstein

*"We may affirm absolutely that nothing great in the world
has been accomplished without passion."*
Hegel

*"So the churches were being strengthened in the faith,
and were increasing in number daily."*
Luke - Acts 16:5 (NASB)

I loved to play basketball. In high school, I had a favorite basketball player I looked up to, and after whom I tried to model my game. I even wore his number—32. I remember two particular games he played. One was a loss and one was a victory. Both had great impact on me.

January 1974, Notre Dame was hosting UCLA. UCLA was led by Bill Walton and Keith Wilkes. UCLA had an 88-game winning streak. Bill Walton hit 12 of 14 shots in this game. He hurt Notre Dame, but did not break them. Notre Dame won 71-70. I was heartbroken! My hero played a good game, but he was not able to get them over the top. The winning streak was broken. It was over! Three years in the making and it was gone in the last tick of the clock.

The other game was the NCAA Championship game in 1973. UCLA played Memphis State. My favorite played perhaps his best game ever. He scored 44 points on 21 of 22 shooting, and if I remember correctly, the only shot he missed was one in which he dunked the ball. Dunking was something you could not do back then. It was goal tending and a missed shot.

My hero's name was Bill Walton. I loved watching him play and seeing him win. His college basketball career was inspiring to me. Impacting the basketball world was never to be my lot in life. I hope to make an impact in Jesus' Kingdom. These two games, UCLA vs. Notre Dame (1974) and UCLA vs. Memphis State (1973) taught me a lot. Life goes on. Bill Walton had a coach named John Wooden. John Wooden was a stoic and a philosopher of a coach. He did not throw chairs or yell at anyone. But he got the best there was out of those who played for him.

All this reminiscing brings home one point. Regardless of the outcome, I need to "play" the best I can and do all I can, but I need a plan. John Wooden always gave his players a plan. We have a plan.

Jesus is very clear on our plan:

John 20:21: "As the Father has sent me, so I am sending you."

Matthew 28:16-20: "But the eleven disciples proceeded to Galilee, to the mountain which Jesus had designated. When they saw Him, they worshiped Him; but some were doubtful. And Jesus came up and spoke to them, saying, 'All authority has been given to Me in heaven and on earth. Go therefore and make disciples of all the nations, baptizing them in the name of the Father and the Son and the Holy Spirit, teaching them to observe all that I commanded you; and lo, I am with you always, even to the end of the age (NASB).'"

This plan was carried out in the book of Acts. The apostles knew the plan, and they were personally informed on more than one occasion (Luke 24, John 20, Acts 1, Matt. 28). They began preaching Jesus and seeing people saved (Acts 2) and then formed the converts into a new church.

I need a regional strategy. Just like Bill Walton played his game according to the game plan given to him, I need to play the game plan given to me. My game plan is best viewed as a regional one: missional and incarnational. I am all about regional plans. I can work in a region and impact as many people as I can in this particular region. My regional plan is a "church-a-day" strategy. It is based on Acts 16:5.

I think national plans for church planting are important. I think regional strategies are either more important or can become the center of traction in a national movement. I define a region as being any area in which I can drive in a two-hour radius. This allows for regional connection in fraternity. We have used the guide of prayer – fraternity – vision. As we have used these three concepts to bring people together, we have found it to be an effective tool to help us gather for a regional connection. This regional focus helps us concentrate our effort and build effective fraternity. It has helped us wrap our arms around our regional goal.

Missional Ecclesiology: Our Churches in America on Mission

The mission of each church in America is to be on point with Jesus' words and make His words and His life our passion. Each church's mission is important and connection to this mission is foundational. Understanding what is formally called missional ecclesiology is important.

The issue of mission is of great theological importance. The missional challenge we face today is enormous. The specific focus is: "How does the church live under Jesus' mission?" This is missional ecclesiology. How does the local church address Jesus' mission? "The church finds itself sharing the gospel with a culture that, on the one hand, is permeated by the heritage of the Enlightenment and modernity and, on the other hand, by postmodern nihilism and hopelessness."[1]

Theologians such as Louis Berkhof tie mission to the resurrection of Jesus Christ. "It is significant that all the appearances of the risen Jesus, with the exception of those on Easter morning itself, contain mandates for the work of missions which is now beginning."[2]

The power of mission lies in the power of God and in the veracity of His message. "When God calls the sinner to accept Christ by faith, he earnestly desires this."[3] In church planting, as in all outreach focuses, the assurance of any success is found in the power of God and the *bona fide* call He extends. The greater understanding of mission's power also lies in our processing the components' relationship to each other. Hirsch is accurate when he says, "*Christology determines missiology, and missiology determines ecclesiology.*"[4] It is in this sense that church must follow mission.[5] Our focus needs this expression: "No church without mission, no mission without church."[6]

Mission is also fueled through God's power. God's omniscience flows to His decree and drawing work in mankind and this makes church planting happen. "The decree of God is His plan for everything."[7] "The Spirit is *missionary;* the Spirit *provides for each disciple;* the Spirit *guides the gathered church.*"[8]

Without missionaries, there would be no Christian faith on earth. In the economy of the gospel, faith depends on hearing the glad tidings, which depends upon someone's being sent, whether from near or far—whether the "beautiful footsteps" of the evangelist who must walk a long distance or only as far as from a neighbor's house (cf. Rom. 10:14f). Here the surprise is that systematic theologians have rarely listed mission among the essential theological doctrines, leaving it aside as only a study of effective methods.[9]

McClendon is correct in focusing our attention on the issue of "sent or sending."[10] "I hope to show that it is exactly by taking up the doctrine of God's Spirit in its relation to mission that we gain clarity about both questions, about our task (mission) and about God's holy nearness (Spirit)."[11] Clarity of our mission is critical. As we come to understand our mission and the missional sending by our Lord, we are able to stay focused on His mission and see His Spirit carry on the work.

Newbigin is correct when he challenges us to stay focused on His mission.[12] He makes clear that the discussion of mission commonly focuses on obedience. While obedience is key and appropriate, to make obedience the primary focus of mission potentially leads us down a path of legalism and mandate. Rather, Newbigin points out the gospel is the essence of any mission we engage, and this mission is not a burden. The obedience focus can tend to make our mission a burden.[13] The Holy Spirit energizes mission. "Where the Spirit is, there mission will flourish."[14]

Further, Newbigin presents the need to see this mission from a Trinitarian perspective. The Father, who holds all things together, is the center of acceptance or rejection. His tender mercies flow all around the mission. Jesus the Son makes repentance and freely-given faith possible. The Holy Spirit drives and orchestrates the mission.[15] Newbigin also drives home the point that mission "is not first of all an action of ours. It is the action of God, the triune God."[16]

Figuring It Out for Mission Today

The idea that "the gospel has penetrated the entire world and the job is almost done" is common in some mission thought today. There can be a sense of colonialism, that is, the age of mission has ended.[17] In fact, the age of mission is in a more dire need than ever. The faulty thinking has, nonetheless, taken a strong hold on the North American church culture. Cole reports that four percent of Southern Baptist churches will plant a new church in their life cycle.[18] If taken as the "norm" for the church in America, then 96 percent of churches in America will not plant a church. Imagine the realistic implications for a society if 96 percent of those able to give birth did not give birth. What would the implications of this type of activity, or lack of activity, produce? The consequences of this thinking and these actions are monumental.[19]

Around the world today God is fueling many church-planting movements that are birthing at least one church a day using human agents with His process in a specific geographical region. Jesus has done so in China, Asia, Africa, Latin America, and many other places except America.[20] This phenomenon is well documented in many sources, including David Garrison:

> As he draws a lost world to himself, Church Planting Movements appear to be the way he is doing it. What began as a small trickle of reports a few years ago has now grown into a steady stream of previously unreached people groups pouring into God's Kingdom.[21]

A church planting movement is defined as "a rapid multiplication of indigenous churches planting churches that sweeps through a people group or population segment."[22] God has burdened my heart to ask Him for such a movement here in Ohio. I believe the most effective means to draw thousands into a regenerating relationship with Jesus Christ is through church planting.[23] In world church planting movements, small churches are the norm and this model is key to our work here in America.[24] The United States is the third largest mission field in the world. Except for Europe, the United States is the only nation in which Christianity is not growing. Each year there are 3,500 churches closing; in 2002 we report only 1,500 churches are planted a year. We are in real need of more and better churches.[25] In 2004, more research indicates 4,000 churches are planted a year in the United States.[26]

As we recognize the great need for church planting, we recognize also that postmodernism brings with it some welcome advantages. Stetzer explains it well:

> In North America today, we have such a rapidly growing and changing population that church planters can't afford to target such a specific niche that we miss one part of a mission field in favor of another. And that's the tricky part, understanding the complicated fabric our society is weaving without becoming overwhelmed.[27]

He further explains: "Missional is the posture – the way in church we approach people in culture—but incarnational describes what's actually happening. Just as Christ came to live among us, we dwell with the people around us."[28]

How Acts Helps Us Figure This Out

The mission of the church is clearly rooted in Jesus' acts and words.[29] Guthrie shows us that Jesus' mission was expressed in two movements. The first is the movement of the kingdom, which formed the foundation of His message and activity. The second movement revolves around His death. The key to Kingdom membership is spiritual. "Since it is spiritual, spiritual qualifications are indispensable."[30] The book of Acts presents the kingdom as key to the preaching message (Acts 19:8; 20:25; 28:23).

Ryrie presents the development of the book of Acts as following the Great Commission. He sees the Great Commission as controlling the entire book, expressing itself at the very beginning in Acts 1:6-8.[31] He further sees the development of the book evidencing the Great Commission's purposes.

> For every reader of Acts has noticed that the first seven chapters concern the work in Jerusalem; chapter 8, the work in Samaria; and the remainder of the book, the uttermost part of the earth.[32]

Jesus expressed His mission to His followers. Their understanding of His mission and purpose is expressly shown by what they did. In the book of Acts, they shared the good news of the gospel and saw people saved. They then took these new converts and formed new churches with them. They planted churches.

The book of Acts shows the death of Jesus to be part of the divine purpose of God.[33] In Acts 2:23 Peter says, "This *Man*, delivered over by the predetermined plan and foreknowledge of God, you nailed to a cross by the hands of godless men and put *Him* to death (NASB)." Peter was careful to juxtapose divine purpose and human responsibility. It is astonishing that the first recorded proclamation of the gospel contains such a reference to both God's foreknowledge and human responsibility.[34]

Acts also shares a key to the message for mission and our understanding of this mission. Acts 20:28 shows the sacrificial nature of Jesus' life and death and the kingdom implications.

> The first disciples were conscious that the community they formed was foreseen and to some extent prepared for by Jesus. We have seen reason to suppose that he himself spoke of the coming *ekklesia*, although the term did not mean an ecclesiastical organization in the sense that it later acquired. The emphasis was on community rather than organization.[35]

91

The book of Acts shows that the early church was community, not organization. The problems that arose only demonstrated the need for organization. All of this is biblical theology directing the understanding of how the church began to be planted. Luke expresses normative disciple-making in four themes: 1) hear the gospel of Jesus Christ so as to repent and trust; 2) be baptized in Jesus' name; 3) receive the Holy Spirit's overwhelming gift; 4) live a consequent life of witness consistent with the Spirit's mission.[36] Success in this mission is to be evaluated by church growth. Newbigin defines "church growth" as "specific activities which are undertaken by human decision to bring the gospel to places or situations where it is not heard, to create a Christian presence in a place or situation where there is no such presence or no effective presence."[37]

On a related theme, Volf offers an interesting definition of church:

> I will join this long tradition by taking Matt. 18:20 as the foundation not only for determining what the church is, but also for how it manifests itself externally as a church. Where two or three are gathered in Christ's name, not only is Christ present among them, but a Christian church is there as well, perhaps a bad church, a church that may well transgress against love and truth, but a church nonetheless.[38]

Neil Cole affirms the same thinking.[39]

> Paul does not use "every person saved" as the criteria for successful mission (Romans 15:23). Paul, who develops mission well in Romans 9-11 and whose chronicle we have in Acts, declares mission is successful when the true meaning of the human story has been disclosed. Because it is the truth, it must be shared universally. It cannot be private opinion…Whenever the gospel is preached the question of the meaning of the human story—the universal story and the personal story of each human being—is posed.[40]

"At the heart of mission is simply the desire to be with him and to give him the service of our lives. At the heart of mission is thanksgiving and praise."[41]

Summary

The church's mission, expressed in missional ecclesiology, drives directly to church planting. The focus and importance of mission is theologically critical. To obey this mission and find its expression today is the obedience factor. As theological mission and Acts' biblical theology are combined, church planting is the outcome from this marriage. The biblical rationale also points our focus to church planting.

The Bible's Direction On This

The biblical rationale drives the focus of church planting in all contexts. God has clearly spoken in both biblical as well as theological realms, driving to careful consideration of church planting as the center of attention. The biblical rationale's focus is on Matthew 16:13-20, Matthew 28:16-20 and Acts 16:5. These passages impact most how church planting is understood. Matthew 16:13-20 begins this focus.

Matthew 16:13-20 Impact on Church Planting

Matthew 16:13-20 states:

> "Now when Jesus came into the district of Caesarea Philippi, He was asking His disciples, 'Who do people say that the Son of Man is?'

> And they said, 'Some say John the Baptist; and others, Elijah; but still others, Jeremiah, or one of the prophets.'

> He said to them, 'But who do you say that I am?'

> Simon Peter answered, 'You are the Christ, the Son of the living God.'

> And Jesus said to him, 'Blessed are you, Simon Barjona, because flesh and blood did not reveal this to you, but My Father who is in heaven.

> I also say to you that you are Peter, and upon this rock I will build My church; and the gates of Hades will not overpower it.

93

> I will give you the keys of the kingdom of heaven; and what-
> ever you bind on earth shall have been bound in heaven,
> and whatever you loose on earth shall have been loosed in
> heaven.'
>
> Then He warned the disciples that they should tell no one
> that He was the Christ (NASB)."

Matthew 16:13-20 contains an incredible revelation: Jesus is going
to build His church, and nothing will get in the way! The structure
and impact of this passage cannot be minimized. The implications
for church planting are clear. Jesus is completely committed to birthing new churches in all regions of the world.

Matthew brings out a key point in this passage. Peter is pin-
pointed by Jesus because of his Christological and Messianic understanding of who Jesus Christ is. It would seem Matthew is grasp-
ing this point from Peter's expression and Jesus' connecting it to the
church building process.[42]

This passage forms the foundation for all church planting. The
"you" in Matthew 16:15 is plural and emphatic, setting the stage for
what is coming. Peter's confession about Jesus' personhood was based
upon divine revelation (Matthew 16:17). Likewise, the building of
the church is uniquely Jesus' job and commitment.[43]

> Jesus' "church" is not the same as his "kingdom:" the two
> words belong to different concepts, the one to "people" and
> the other to "rule" or "reign." But neither must they be op-
> posed to each other, as if both cannot occupy the same place
> in time. The messianic reign is calling out the messianic
> people. The kingdom has been inaugurated; the people are
> being gathered.[44]

The power involved in the "church" itself is uniquely announced. In
Matthew 16:19 Matthew uses a periphrastic construction, specifically a periphrastic future perfect tense. It does not mean "will be"
but "will have been." "Thus God will not ratify at the last judgment
what Peter does in the present age, but Peter does in the present age
what God has already determined."[45] This is a powerful affirmation
of what our mission focus must be.

Matthew 28:16-20 Impact on Church Planting

Matthew 28:16-20 states:

"But the eleven disciples proceeded to Galilee, to the mountain which Jesus had designated.

When they saw Him, they worshiped Him; but some were doubtful.

And Jesus came up and spoke to them, saying, 'All authority has been given to Me in heaven and on earth.

Go therefore and make disciples of all the nations, baptizing them in the name of the Father and the Son and the Holy Spirit, teaching them to observe all that I commanded you; and lo, I am with you always, even to the end of the age (NASB).'"

The Great Commission in Matthew 28 is also central to our understanding of church planting. There are five Great Commission passages: Matthew 28:16-20, Mark 16:14ff, Luke 24:46-49, John 20:19-23 and Acts 1:6-8. Matthew is unique because of its time, place, and previous reference as Jesus spoke to His disciples before He died. Jesus "set" an appointment with His disciples before He died to meet them in Galilee, the location of Matthew's Great Commission (Matthew 26:32; 28:7). Matthew's account gives the summary of this appointment. This Great Commission was the last word the disciples and apostles received. Acts clearly shows what they did with the Great Commission. They shared the gospel and birthed new churches with new disciples.

Hence, the Great Commission in Matthew 28:16-20 lays a profound foundation for church planting. In the context of worship (Matt. 28:17), the disciples and others who were there were instructed to make disciples (Matt. 28:19). They were given the supporting vision in which to make disciples, which was to go, baptize (immerse them in water in light of the Trinitarian focus), and teach them to obey all that Jesus had said.

Every Christian is commissioned, like Jesus at his baptism, to be a missionary. This is made explicit in the Great Commission (e.g., in Matt. 28:19f. [cf. Mark 16:15ff]; Acts 1:8), a marching order that by the Baptist vision applies to every disciple now as it did then. To be missionaries is to proclaim in our words and by our lives that Jesus is the Christ, the Savior of the world, so that "all nations" are summoned to a like discipleship. Though the task is difficult and costly, those who obey it are promised power from on high: they will be equipped by God's Spirit to give their witness and to bear its cost.[46]

How God works: Acts 16:5 – Party time!

My wife and I have a date we celebrate each year (other than our anniversary). This day is the day that God provided the last of the money necessary for our two kids' college costs be paid off! This happened about 10 years before we thought it would, but it did happen! When Jesus sent the last amount of money we needed, we were overwhelmed and exhilarated in seeing God move so powerfully in our personal world. He provided the necessary money six months before the school loans were set to begin collection. This was so profound that I have the day marked on the calendar on my computer, so when that day comes, I know exactly when it is. We party!

Jesus said a lot about building His church (Matthew 16 and 28, for example). He empowers His people to carry out His mission (Acts 1, for example). So, it makes perfect sense that He would plant a church a day, even more than one a day! We have that record in Acts 16:5.

Acts 16:5 is a profoundly important verse for our consideration. Here Luke states: "So the churches were being strengthened in the faith, and were increasing in number daily (NASB)." We have examined the motivation behind church planting as expressed in Matthew 16:13-20 and Matthew 28:16-20. These motivational thoughts are critical to an accurate understanding of missional ecclesiology.

Stetzer and Bird are right when they describe Paul's journeys as "church planting journeys."[47] We have all been taught that Paul was on missionary journeys. We have been taught correctly, but perhaps not fully. We do well to describe Paul's work by the fruit of his work and not by the work alone. The fruit of his work was the formation of new churches; this fruit came from the missional work he was engaging.

Acts 16:5, on the other hand, is a clear expression of Matthew 16:13-20 and Matthew 28:16-20's impact on the leaders of the early church. God used this understanding and motivation to form a church a day movement of church planting in Asia Minor. As a summary verse, we need to carefully examine all Luke is telling us. Let us begin with a diagrammatical examination.

My conclusion has already been stated. I plan to demonstrate it by showing: 1) A diagram of Acts 16:5; 2) A look at the specific words Luke uses to describe church growth in the book of Acts; 3) A look at some specific wording, called lexicography; and 4) Look at some grammar. These four areas will impact our understanding of Acts 16:5.

Summary Observations – Greek and English Diagrams

Do you remember middle school English grammar? There we were all exposed to this thing called diagrammatical analysis or using lines to break apart a sentence to better understand how each part comes together. We need to do this with Acts 16:5 to achieve the most understanding we can get.

In its most simple form, a line diagram of Acts 16:5 is significantly important.

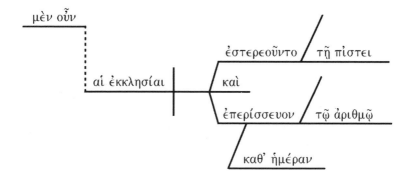

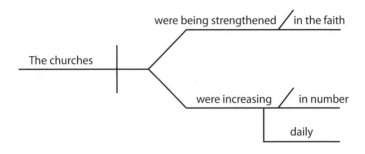

Based on this diagram, we ask, "What do we do with the singular subject (the word "churches" is plural, but it is one subject with two verbs) and compound verbs?" Whatever conclusions we might draw from Acts 16:5, the fact of a singular subject with the compound verbs is exegetically demanding. The double statements made by the verbs are about churches in Asia Minor, not individuals in Asia Minor. Luke is careful to keep the subject and reference point of his growth statements clear: when he talks about individuals, they are individuals; when he talks about churches, they are groups of people who are called a church. This becomes clearer as we compare passages.

Foundational to our understanding of the importance of Acts 16:5, and the impact of the passage on church planting thought, is that this verse is considered a summary verse. Longenecker points out:

> This summary statement…is comparable to the summary statements of 6:7; 9:31 and 12:24 that culminate their respective panels of material. Introduced by Luke's favorite connective men oun (see comments on 1:6), it stresses the strengthening and growth of the churches as a result of Paul's missionary policy and the response of the Jerusalem church to it.[48]

Commenting on Acts 16:5, F. F. Bruce says, "What is perhaps the most crucial phase of Luke's narrative is now brought to a conclusion with a characteristic report of progress."[49] His conclusion is profound. As I contemplate the importance of this particular verse in Acts, I need to make sure I understand Acts 16:5's importance. It is a clearly focused statement Luke makes about God's birthing of churches in Asia Minor. God is planting at least one new church each day in this part of Asia Minor.

Luke's Use of Specific Terminology

Luke is saying something different in Acts 16:5 because of his choice of terminology. If he is trying to talk about growth of individuals in the local church, why would he shift from what he had said on more than one occasion to this new expression? Since Acts 16:5 is a summary verse, Luke's use of differing terms is even more important. He has used five other words to describe what God was doing in Acts. In Acts 16:5 he chooses a different term.

The five words are:

- Acts 2:41, 47; 5:14; 11:24 "added" – *prostithemi*
- Acts 6:7, 9:31, 12:24 "continued to increase" – *plethuno*
- Acts 11:21; 9:35 "turned" – *epistrepho*
- Acts 13:48 "appointed" – *tasso*
- Acts 19:26 "turned away" – *methistemi*

Luke chooses to use *perisseuo* ("increasing") in Acts 16:5 and not prostithemi. Why the shift? Some say he is mixing it up to change style, tired of the other way of writing. Perhaps, but I am unconvinced. I am not comfortable dismissing this important verse as simply a change in style, especially since Acts 16:5 is a summary verse.

Luke's habit in growth passages is to reference individuals:

- Acts 2:41 – "So then, those who had received his word were baptized; and that day there were added (*prostithemi*) about three thousand souls." 3,000 souls is the subject, a clear reference to individuals.

- Acts 2:47 - "And the Lord was adding (*prostithemi*) to their number day by day those who were being saved." The Lord was adding the ones being saved – clear reference to individuals.

- Acts 5:14 - "And all the more believers in the Lord, multitudes of men and women, were constantly added (*prostithemi*) to their number." Men and women are the multitudes being added.

- Acts 6:7 - "The word of God kept on spreading; and the number of the disciples continued to increase greatly (*plethuno*) in Jerusalem, and a great many of the priests were becoming obedient to the faith." Disciples were increasing in Luke's account here. A reference to individuals.

- Acts 9:35 - "And all who lived at Lydda and Sharon saw him, and they turned (*epistrepho*) to the Lord." Here, Luke tells us the individuals who lived in Lydda and Sharon turned to Jesus Christ, another reference to individuals.

- Acts 11:21-24 - "And the hand of the Lord was with them, and a large number who believed turned (*epistrepho*) to the Lord. The news about them reached the ears of the church at Jerusalem, and they sent Barnabas off to Antioch. Then when he arrived and witnessed the grace of God, he rejoiced and began to encourage them all with resolute heart to remain true to the Lord; for he was a good man, and full of the Holy Spirit and of faith. And considerable numbers were brought (*prostithemi*) to the Lord." The believers, a large number, turned to the Lord—another reference to individuals.

- Acts 12:24 - "But the word of the Lord continued to grow and to be multiplied (*plethuno*)." In this verse, Luke tells us the word of the Lord was the growth point—not a reference to individual believers, but to the tool used to bring the growth.

- Acts 13:48-49 - "When the Gentiles heard this, they began rejoicing and glorifying the word of the Lord; and as many as had been appointed (*tasso*) to eternal life believed. And the word of the Lord was being spread through the whole region." As many as had been appointed believed—another reference to individuals.

- Acts 16:5 - "So the churches were being strengthened in the faith, and were increasing (*perisseuo*) in number daily." Acts 16:5 has churches as the subject—not a reference to an individual.

- Acts 9:31 - "So the church throughout all Judea and Galilee and Samaria enjoyed peace, being built up; and going on in the fear of the Lord and in the comfort of the Holy Spirit, it continued to increase (*plethuno*)." This verse likewise has church as its subject.

• Acts 19:26 - "You see and hear that not only in Ephesus, but in almost all of Asia, this Paul has persuaded and turned away (*methistemi*) a considerable number of people, saying that gods made with hands are no gods at all." This summary shows another reference to individuals becoming believers: a large number, but another reference to individuals.

Luke's use of churches in Acts 16:5 as the subject shows he is not thinking of individual people. In other growth passages Luke does not use churches (*ecclesia*) as the subject (except 9:31). He keeps the individual reference when he wishes to talk about growth of individual believers.

Luke makes a distinction between the word "church" in Acts and the individuals who make up the church. When he wished to talk about individuals, he did so with individual references. Luke changed this when he made churches the subject in Acts 16:5.

Lexical Information

A simple look at the lexicon helps provide perspective. *Prostithemi* means "to add something to an existing quantity – 'to add.'"[50] Another example: "to add something that is already present or exists."[51]

Plethuno means "continue to increase." Louw and Nida say, "to increase greatly in number or extent—'to grow, to increase greatly, to multiply.'"[52] BAGD adds "to cause to become greater in number trans. and be multiplied, grow, increase pass."[53]

Perisseuo "increasing," which Louw and Nida tell us means "to be or exist in abundance, with the implication of being considerably more than what would be expected 'to abound, to be in abundance, to be a lot of, to exist in a large quantity, to be left over.'"[54] BAGD tells us it means "grow."[55] "The common Pauline sense 'have abundance' survives in MGr (MGr = Modern Greek)."[56]

Perhaps we can express it this way, from this lexical information: *perisseuo* is a word of multiplication while *prostithemi* is a word of addition. Luke intentionally changes the word to communicate that something different is going on in this passage. We also see in Luke's statement in Acts 9:31 that we might consider *plethuno* a word that is middle ground compared to *prostithemi* "to add" and *perisseuo* "to multiply." It may represent a flowing continuum, which might look like this:

Figure 1.3. Lexical continuum flow

prostithemi, methistemi, epistrepho, tasso → plethuno → perisseuo

Luke uses *prostithemi, methistemi, epistrepho,* and *tasso* as words of general addition or words of individual progression. The progressions might be great in terms of fruit (PTL) but, in comparison, is not the expansion that the other expressions are.

Could we consider that Luke is pressing the concept of church growth with just such a continuum? When Luke wishes to focus on concepts of addition he uses *prostithemi, methistemi, epistrepho,* and *tasso*; when he wishes to speak of greater growth, he uses *plethuno*; and when he talks about multiplication, he uses *perisseuo*.

Another Grammatical Consideration in Acts 16:5

The use of the imperfect tense with both verbs *estereounto* (strengthened) and *eperisseuon* (increasing) in Acts 16:5 is of great interest. Dan Wallace calls them iterative imperfects. Wallace says:

> The imperfect is frequently used for repeated action in past time. It is similar to the customary imperfect, but it is not something that regularly recurs. Further, the iterative imperfect occurs over a shorter span of time. There are two types of iterative imperfect: (1) Iterative proper, in which the imperfect indicates repeated action by the same agent; and (2) Distributive, in which the imperfect is used for individual acts of multiple agents. . . .Many grammarians make no distinction between the iterative and the customary imperfect. However, while the customary is repeated action in past time, it has two elements that the iterative imperfect does not have: (1) regularly recurring action (or, action at regular intervals),

and (2) action that tends to take place over a long span of time. Thus, in some sense, it might be said that the customary imperfect is a subset of the iterative imperfect. The difference between these two will be seen more clearly via the illustrations. Often the gloss *kept on doing, going,* etc. helps the student to see the force of this use of the imperfect, but this is not always the case, especially with distributive imperfects. Another gloss is *repeatedly, continuously doing.*[57]

What Wallace's observation means is the actions of both verbs is repeatedly and continuously ongoing. Thus, the churches in this section of Asia Minor were both continually growing in strength and also growing in number each day. This use of the imperfect also matches my thesis that something unique is occurring in Acts 16:5. I translate the key phrase this way: "God was repeatedly multiplying churches" not individuals.

Summary

Theological and biblical rationales lead me to conclude our mission is critical and must influence our church life and thinking. Mission has many expressions in the local church. One key expression is to plant churches so the gospel can penetrate the community and tell God's story to all. We do well to follow the example laid down for us by the early church. The early church received Jesus' Great Commission, and they proceeded to plant churches. This church planting process developed to a new church each day in Asian Minor as reported in Acts 16:5. The theological rationale drives missional ecclesiology, culminating in church planting.

Both Matthew 16:13-20 and Matthew 28:16-20 inform our understanding of church planting. Jesus' expression is demonstrated in Acts as fuel for church planting. Acts 16:5, as a summary verse, also directs our understanding of church planting. Jesus did indeed plant a church a day in Asia Minor.

What would this look like in a region? Let us take a region like Ohio that has a driving diameter of two hours—in other words, two hours of driving can connect most people involved at a central point.

In Ohio, we are seeing 70-80 new churches a year (2011). A church a day in Ohio would go something like this: We beseech the Lord of the harvest for workers in and from the harvest to move that number of churches planted from 70-80 to 360-370 a year. Asking God to do this among His churches that preach His Gospel is what we focus on. This would require having strategic regional meetings among those churches preaching His Gospel to join together for prayer, conversation, and relationship building; looking for ways to pray more effectively and learn from each other how to improve our church planting works in a church family application.

Notes

[1]Karkkainen, *An Introduction to Ecclesiology,* 158

[2]Berkhof, *Systematic theology,* 1979, 320

[3]Berkhof, *Systematic Theology,* 462

[4]Hirsch, *The Forgotten Ways,* 142; emphasis Hirsch

[5]Ibid, 143

[6]Karkkainen, *An Introduction to Ecclesiology,* 159

[7]Ryrie, *Basic Theology,* 311

[8]Karkkainen, *An Introduction to Ecclesiology,* 159

[9]McClendon, *Doctrine: Systematic Theology,* 417

[10]Ibid, 417

[11]Ibid, 418

[12]Newbigin, *The Gospel in a Pluralistic Society,* 116

[13]Newbigin 1992, 116-117

[14]McClendon, *Doctrine: Systematic Theology,* 436-437

[15]Newbigin 1992, 118

[16]Newbigin 1992, 135

[17]McClendon, *Doctrine: Systematic Theology,* 424

[18]Hirsch, *The Forgotten Ways,* 139

[19]Cole, *Organic Church,* 119

[20]Garrison, *Church Planting Movements,* 35

[21]Ibid, 16; emphasis Garrison

[22]Ibid, 21

[23]Ibid, 28; Wagner, *Church Planting for a Greater Harvest,* 11

[24]McIntosh, *One Size Doesn't Fit All,* 17

[25]Nebel, *Big Dreams in Small Places,* 97-98

[26]Smith, *Church Planting Overview,* p. 3

[27]Stetzer, *Planting Missional Churches,* 1

[28]Stetzer, *Planting Missional Churches,* 2

[29]Carson, Moo and Morris, *An Introduction to the New Testament,* 182

[30]Guthrie, *New Testament Theology,* 408

[31]Ryrie, *Basic Theology,* 104

[32]Ibid, 104-105

[33]Guthrie, *New Testament Theology,* 461

[34]Ibid, 461

[35]Ibid, 732

[36]McClendon, *Doctrine: Systematic Theology,* 437

[37]Newbigin 1992, 121

[38]Volf, *After Our Likeness,* 136

[39]Cole, *Organic Church,* 99ff

[40]Newbigin 1992, 125

[41]Newbigin 1992, 127

[42]Carson, "Matthew," *Expositor's Bible Commentary,* 8:364

[43]Ibid, 8:365-368

[44]Ibid, 8:369-370

[45]Gundry 1982, 335

[46]McClendon, *Doctrine: Systematic Theology,* 419

[47]Stetzer and Bird, *Viral Churches,* 21

[48]Longnecker, *John-Acts. The Expositor's Bible Commentary,* 9:456

[49]Bruce, *Commentary on the book of Acts,* 324

[50]Louw and Nida, *Greek-English Lexicon of the New Testament Based on Semantic Domains,* 602

[51]Bauer, Arndt, Gingrich, and Danker, *A Greek-English Lexicon of the New Testament and Other Early Christian Literature,* Second Edition, 718-719

[52]Louw and Nida 1989, 602

[53]Bauer, Arndt, Gingrich, and Danker, , 669

[54]Louw and Nida 1989, 600

[55]Bauer, Arndt, Gingrich, and Danker, 650-651

[56]Moulton and Milligan, *The Vocabulary of the Greek Testament,* 508

[57]Wallace, *Greek Grammar Beyond the Basics*, 546-547

Chapter 7

WE ARE IN GOOD COMPANY: FOCUSING ON THE ENTIRE HARVEST

"Tell me what you're laughing at and I shall tell you who you are."
Goethe

"All great achievements require time."
David Joseph Schwartz

"Just as the Father sent me, I send you."
Jesus Christ

Jesus commanded us to go and make disciples of all people groups, "immersing them in the name of the Father and the name of the Son and the name of the Holy Spirit; do not worry, I am with you until the end of the age" (Matthew 28:19-20).

Jesus had set the foundation through His example of how to go about doing this. Through His regular healing of people He comes to what we know as Matthew 9 and 11 to give us key direction.

In Matthew 9:35-39, Matthew shares with us: "Jesus was going through all the cities and villages, teaching in their synagogues and proclaiming the gospel of the kingdom, and healing every kind of disease and every kind of sickness. Seeing the people, He felt compassion for them, because they were distressed and dispirited like sheep without a shepherd. Then He said to His disciples, 'The harvest is plentiful, but the workers are few.' Therefore beseech the Lord of the harvest to send out workers into His harvest.'"

In Matthew 11:28-30, Matthew says: "Come to Me, all who are weary and heavy-laden, and I will give you rest. Take My yoke upon you and learn from Me, for I am gentle and humble in heart, and *you will find rest for your souls.* For My yoke is easy and My burden is light."

These passages set a powerful tone for how to address and care for people—all people—regardless of where they live. Jesus' habit was to travel the region and keep the mission foremost on His mind and the minds of those he was discipling and reaching (Mark 1:35-39; Matthew 4:23-25; Mark 7:31 for example).

Paul had his own experience with Jesus in his own personal training time with Him in the desert. Galatians tells us that Paul learned his gospel presentation through "revelation of Jesus Christ." (Galatians 1:12) This revelation was the foundation of what he did and said for his life - definitely for the time prior to arriving to "equal" status with the other apostles (described in Galatians 2:1). This is to say that Paul was directly instructed by Jesus on what the gospel was about and also directly instructed by Jesus on His method—I believe no different than our method—Jesus used Matthew 28:19-20 with Paul.

As we look at Paul's first missionary journey beginning in Acts 13:1 with his divine commissioning, what did his methodology look like? In other words, what cities did he go to and what cities did he intentionally bypass? Did he intentionally bypass any city? Was Paul all-inclusive in his sites of presenting the gospel since all were in great need, or was he more selective, going to the cities of higher density first and the other cities after that?

Our journey here is to explore Paul's approach to his incarnational missionality that led to a church a day in Asia Minor (Acts 16:5). What was behind his decisions in that phase of God's work for this region? We have already explored all the pieces that led to a church a day in central Asia Minor (chapter 6) and our work here is to explore as best we can what Paul was thinking as he engaged Jesus' mission. Can we break down his methodological considerations?

We all stand upon someone else's shoulders here in the West doing our church planting, and so did Paul. Jesus had done so much already. How do we engage the harvest today? How would we define "balanced" when it comes to church planting? Do we only focus on population density and metropolitan areas, or do we engage everyplace and work to have the multiple methodologies and tools to accomplish such an effort? Paul will help us answer this question as we examine his methodology in his pre-Acts 16:5 work.

I personally am blessed by those who focus uniquely on densely populated urban centers. We must do that. But we must have a focus on all of the harvest as well. Did Paul focus on the entire harvest? Jesus did spend time blanketing the countryside with His presence and ministry work as well as the main urban centers of Israel in His day—Jerusalem vs. Capernaum, Bethsaida, or Nazareth.

Acts gives us this list of cities recorded in Acts 13 and 14:

- Salamis - 13:5 (Paul began in the Jewish synagogue)
- Paphos - 13:6
- Perga - Acts 13:13
- Pisidian Antioch - Acts 13:14 (Paul also focused on the synagogue there.)

Here Paul decides to turn to the Gentiles and the whole region hears the gospel - 13:46-49.

- Iconium - 14:1
- Lycaonia - 14:6
- Lystra - 14:8
- Derbe - 14:10
- Pamphylia - 14:24
- Perga - 14:25
- Attalia - 14:25

What kind of cities were they? How do they help us understand Paul's understanding of his mission as given by Jesus? How many smaller cities, in Bible times standards, are there vs. larger, major cities? Did Paul frequent the smaller cities or just any city that was next on the road he was traveling?

Many factors influence the spread of the gospel. Attempting to draw from common presumption on Christianity's spread by sociologists and theologians, I work to see how much of Paul's strategy we can infer in answering the question at hand: how inclusive was Paul's mindset on spreading the gospel to various size cities? Was he holistic toward the prepared harvest or selective based on population rates or density of population?

We begin by reporting what we do know about the size of the cities named in Acts 13 and 14 and see what this information brings to us. From there we explore what it means to us today as we have conversation about where to go next.

Chandler (from whom Stark builds his list) lists the largest 22 Roman cities 100 CE. Those listed in Asian Minor are:

- Ephesus - 200,000
- Antioch - 150,000
- Pergamum - 120,000
- Smyrna - 75,000[1]

None of these are listed in Paul's first missionary journey, though Paul left from Antioch to head out. These were known to Paul and eventually came to his missional focus, but on his first missionary journey, he did not go that far.

Sociological Considerations for Expansion

A survey of relevant sociological premises for Christianity's growth is relevant and helpful for us as we grapple with this chapter's questions. This survey can dovetail with the rest of our consideration about city size and Paul's potential mindset for mission. Our goal is to work at discovering what was on Paul's mind as he embraced the mission the Holy Spirit placed on him in Acts 13.

Longenecker tells us, "As Paul and Barnabas left Pisidian Antioch, therefore, they were faced with a choice as to the future directions of their mission. Choosing the southeastern route (of Galatia), they headed off to what would become a ministry to people of three very different types of cities in the southern portion of the Roman province of Galatia."[2]

Spreading of the Gospel

Adolph von Harnack succinctly shares a key thought in using the notion of the *expansion* of Christianity; in order to rise, a movement must spread. God is behind the spread and that God would use sociological matters to cause spread is a very real possibility. Our focus is on Paul's understanding of the gospel spreading, looking at his focus on missional ecclesiology.

More Urban the More Accepting of Deviant Subcultures

Sociologically, one key consideration is this: "The more urban the place, the higher the rate of unconventionality."[3] Fischer's thesis is that the larger the population, in absolute numbers, the easier it is to assemble a "critical mass" needed to form a deviant subculture. Here he specifically includes deviant religious movements. During the period in question, Christianity obviously qualified as a deviant religious movement in that it clearly was at variance with prevailing religious norms of Paul's day. Therefore, Fischer's theory of urbanism predicts that Christians would have assembled the critical mass needed to form a church sooner in the larger cities.[4]

Cultural Continuity

Stark makes the point that cultural consistency contributes to the acceptance of something new.

"Specifically, people are more willing to adopt a new religion to the extent that it retains cultural continuity with conventional religion(s) with which they already are familiar." For, as Arthur Darby Nock (1933:9) put it, "The receptivity of most people for that which is wholly new (if anything is) is small."[5]

The first is cultural continuity. Not only was Christianity highly continuous with the Jewish heritage of diasporan Jews, it also was highly congruent with their Hellenic cultural elements. The second proposition is that social movements recruit primarily on the basis of interpersonal attachments that exist, or *form, between the convert* and *members of the group*. In effect, people accept a new religion because their friends and relatives lead them to it (Lofland and Stark, 1965; Stark and Bainbridge, 1980, 1985, 1987). Who were the friends and relatives of the early Christian missionaries setting out from Jerusalem to spread their faith? The Jews of the diaspora, of course. In fact, many of the missionaries were, like Paul himself, diasporan Jews.[6]

Paul's first stop was commonly the synagogue. Since the gospel was going to new places wherever Paul went, we can see the culture continuity as significant to his method, particularly the work in the synagogues.

Acts 13:46 records that Paul was now going to the Gentiles exclusively. This would cut down on the connection to this concept, except that Paul continued to visit the synagogues (Acts 17:1, 10, 17; 18:4, 7, 8, 17, 19, 26; 19:8). It would make his method more focused on the traveling ease as well as the urban subculture. But, as Paul focused on smaller cities, in terms of population, this would counter against this thought. This turn to the Gentiles would at least mean Paul's focus at Pisidian Antioch was more toward the Gentiles. Paul kept the synagogue as a key contact-making strategy. Could it be that Paul's method was this idea: the smaller the city, the greater the need to focus on the Diasporan help (synagogue) and Hellenism's contribution?

The cities Paul visited on his first missionary journey were not the largest cities in Asia Minor. They were connected by ease of travel, i.e. roads. In the midst of this missionary journey Paul moved to focus on the Gentiles, but did not abandon the cultural, diasporan connection through the synagogue. The synagogue would still be used for the growth of Christianity. Paul followed one Roman road on his first missionary journey once he left Cyprus. It is called Via Sebaste road built by Augustus in 6 BC (Sebaste is the Greek equivalent to Augustus).

Are we able to accept the concept that the primary point Paul and company had on their mind was choosing a road and following it? How missional was that? How does this concept impact us as we explore our missional realities?

Stark presents some interesting hypotheses relating to the expansion of Christianity and the church's presence in Asian cities in 100 CE and also in 180 CE. I am more concerned with 50 CE, not so much 100 or 180 CE. In exploring Stark's thoughts, consider how his thoughts help in exploring a missional, exploratory system for church planting.

Stark does a good job of presenting the growth of Christianity from its inception to AD 350. He follows a 3.4 percent growth idea, and this growth would chart like this:

Year	Number of Christians	Percent of Roman Population
40	1,000	-
50	1,397	-
100	7,434	-
150	39,560	0.07
180	107,863	0.18
200	210,516	0.35
250	1,120,246	1.9
300	5,961,290	9.9
312	8,904,032	14.8
350	31,722,489	52.9

From a differing perspective, Alan Hirsch shares an intriguing experience he had at a seminar on missional church. At this seminar, the leader asked, "How many Christians do you think there were in the year AD 100?" then quickly followed with, "How many Christians do you thin there were just before Constantine came on the scene, say, AD 310?" The answer is powerful. In AD 100 there were an estimated 25,000 Christians. In AD 310, it is estimated there were 20 million Christians.[7]

Though written differently from Hirsh's perspective as reported elsewhere in this book, a growth to 31 million believers by 350 CE is impressive, especially if that number constituted more than 50 percent of the Roman population! (Stark is basing the last column on a Roman Empire population figure of 60 million).

Pauline Strategy

To further support this growth concept, Stark gives these key ideas:

- The closer a city was to Jerusalem, the more likely it was to have a Christian church.

- Port cities had more churches in them sooner than non-port cities.

- Hellenic cities had Christian congregations sooner than non-Hellenic cities.

- He begins his thinking by saying that larger cities had Christian congregations sooner than smaller cities.[8]

Stark's conclusion was this; "Paul concentrated on the more Hellenized cities; Paul tended to missionize port cities; Paul tended to missionize cities with substantial Jewish Diasporan communities; Cities missionized by Paul had churches sooner than cities Paul did not visit; Cities with a significant Diasporan community were Christianized sooner than other cities."[9]

My understanding of Stark's work is this: Stark does say that city size was important in church expansion. He said, "The data shows a substantial difference: three-fourths of the larger cities had a church by 100 CE, while only a third of smaller cities did so. All the larger cities had a church by 180 CE, but a third of the small cities still did not."[10] A key part of Stark's research of his hypothesis about city size and its influence on church expansion was his look at two other "religious" expansions - both mystical and pagan: Cybele and Isis. He does conclude for both of these explorations that city size was not significant for either of these worship systems and their expansion.[11] What this means is Stark's own premise is not supported by his research.

He adds: "The historical record strongly supports the idea that Cybelene worship and Isiacism served as important stepping-stones to Christianity by shaping pagan culture in ways that made the Christ story more familiar and credible."[12]

From an expansion perspective, Stark presents the idea that "Other things being equal, a new *religion is more likely to grow to the degree that it sustains continuity with the religious culture of those being missionized.*"[13]

It seems that for Paul's strategy to be explored and dissected, attempting to analyze his strategy by his actions, there were at least four positive contributing factors to his pathway that help us understand how Paul went about pursuing his mission:

- Port Cities
- Hellenized Cities

116

- Diasporan Communities
- Roman Roads/Ship Pathways.

Port Cities: Stark does a good job of demonstrating the importance of Paul's stopping in port cities. There was so much ship traffic in the Roman empire that the port city did come to have key stopping points.

Longenecker comments: "So Luke's mention of Attalia here probably has no more significance than his mention of Seleucia (13:4), the port of Syrian Antioch, and merely identifies the place of embarkation for the voyage back to Syria."[14]

I share this because it appears Longenecker has connection with my contention. Though churches did spawn in port cities by 100 and 180 CE, in 50 CE Paul's focus was elsewhere in his initial thinking.

Hellenized Cities: Hellenism is so important because more Jews spoke Greek than Hebrew or Aramaic and nearly all the Jews of the Diaspora spoke Greek. "This gains support from the fact that Nazareth was located only several miles from Sapphores, the capital of Galilee and a sophisticated Greek speaking city."[15] This, combined with the Scriptures being written in Greek, supports this concept.

Diasporan Communities: The Jewish communities of the Diaspora also worshiped in Greek. They did this over against the ethnic barriers their religion placed on them. Hellenism also was very conducive to accommodating "new gods" in their systems. These all bring strong support to persuading others to a new thought - Jesus Christ.[16]

We also know that the communities Paul travelled to in the Greek Eastern empire were comprised of perhaps as high as 10 percent Jewish population.[17] Meeks also supports this size of Jewish population in the cities Paul visited in the Greek east, even suggesting as high as 15 percent.[18]

Roman Roads: As Meeks puts it, "the people of the Roman Empire traveled more extensively and more easily than anyone before them—or would again until the nineteenth century."[19]

Though it is easy to think that travel was difficult in Paul's day, it just was not so. As a matter of fact, to see that travel has only recently been more available is profound and energizing when it comes to thinking about the spread of the gospel. Paul had many travel tools at his disposal.

Though travel was better than ever before, the Roman road was far from perfect. Roman roads were too small for wagons and most travelled on the side of the road in the dirt because the road was too hard on feet and legs when dry and slippery when wet. Hills were too steep for wagons and they did not build bridges. Boats were what made Roman empire accessible.[20]

"From the schematic itineraries of the book of Acts alone, Ronald Hock has calculated that Paul traveled nearly 10,000 miles during his reported career ..."[21] Meeks also adds: "Roman power made possible this flourishing travel in two very practical ways: the Roman military presence undertook to keep brigandage on the land and piracy on the sea to a minimum, and the imperial government took responsibility for a road system throughout its regions."[22]

Charlesworth estimates that travel by sea in Paul's day could cover 100 miles a day; 25 - 30 miles a day by horse (using fresh horses); 15-20 miles a day walking - at most.[23]

If this thinking is correct, Paul's primary thinking was eased by the direction of the Roman road. On this Roman road, Paul met Hellenized areas with strong Diasporan communities. It seems that Paul was blessed to be involved in a time when any place was good for him, but these areas in southern Turkey proved better. These roads were increasingly important particularly in the mountainous areas of modern day Turkey—specifically southern Turkey.

French is clear that the Roman road Sebaste was the driving force to Paul's first missionary journey. He writes:

> Is there a correlation between the then existing Roman roads and the routes of Paul's journey? For the first journey (?AD 46-48), certainly. The existence of a paved Roman road, the *via Sebaste* (built 6 BC), leading up from Pamphylia to Antiochia in Pisidia and Iconium in Lycaonia and starting (as is now demonstrated by milestone evidence) precisely at Perge, suggest that Paul deliberately took the easiest, most convenient, and perhaps the only route into Asian Minor, to the

colonies of Antiochia and Iconium where there were Jewish communities (Acts 13:14 Antiochia and 14:1 Iconium).[24]

French does, interestingly enough, hypothesize that Paul rejected the major Roman roads in the second and third missionary journeys because of his desire to stay away from the political problems he saw coming which he experienced at Antioch (Acts 13:50) and Lystra (Acts 14:19ff).[25]

We do not have record of Paul preaching in the "countryside." We see that Jesus did. "Paul was a city person. The city breathes through his language. Jesus' parables of sowers and weeds, sharecroppers, and mud-roofed cottages call forth smells of manure and earth, and the Aramaic of the Palestinian villages often echoes in the Greek."[26] "Despite the fact that about 95 percent of its population lived on farms or in tiny rural villages, Rome was an urban empire."[27]

There was a symbiotic relationship between the city and countryside but the power was in the city. "The conservatism of the villages preserved their diversity; changes in the city were in the direction of a common Greco-Roman culture. This was most obvious in language."[28]

Stark's thought that Rome was overwhelmingly non-city, yet Rome was an urban empire, is an interesting thought. The power of the city—of any size—rises to the top of our consideration. If the population we are exploring is mostly non-city dwellers, yet one of Rome's greater traits was the urban nature of her empire, then the nature of a city of any size is critically important. It would be in this environment that the political power, the financial power, etc. would all reside. This would help us understand why and how Paul developed his strategy: ***Go to a city of any size.*** Where the Roman roads went, the city developed. Where the Roman road went, Paul went. Where the city of any size was on the Roman road also meant the confluence of the smaller villages and countrysides.

We can add to this Paul's well-known thought: Romans 15:20 "And thus I aspired to preach the gospel, not where Christ was already named, so that I would not build on another man's foundation (NASB)." As we embrace this as key to Paul's thinking, combined with the Roman road system, we are well on the way to understanding how Paul explored his mission and had it work out in history in Acts. He clearly used Diasporan communities and Hellenized communities as his focus.

The reasons why the city was key are: language was common; the city used common forms for life; they used like inscriptions; they used stereotyped phrases common to city life (councils announced decrees; clubs honored patrons, bereaved commemorated their dead, etc.)[29]

Longenecker adds: "Evidently Luke was more interested in the illustrious Phrygian cities of Antioch and Iconium than in the smaller Lycaonian towns of Lystra and Derbe. Probably the larger and more influential churches were in Antioch and Iconium as well, though the congregations in the smaller and more rural towns seem to have contributed more young men as candidates for the missionary endeavor, e.g. Timothy from Lystra (16:1-3; 20:4); Gaius from Derbe (20:4)—a pattern not altogether different from today, where the larger churches often capture the headlines and the smaller congregations provide much of the personnel."[30]

On the Heels of "One a Day"

In Acts 6:6-10, we have the days after Paul experiencing God planting a church a day in that part of Asia Minor. Missional discovery— beyond our attempt to discern Paul's motivation for his strategy— also has a key divine involvement.

In Acts 16 we have Paul being told on two occasions (Acts 16:6-7) by the Holy Spirit and the Spirit of Jesus to not go there. We then have Paul receiving a vision that makes clear his expansion westward so that he travels to Macedonia.

We see in Paul's further work westward that he keeps the same method of operation in forming missional communities. He does follow both the Roman roads and ship courses; he stays focused on Hellenized cities and diasporan communities.

This chapter has created a tension, if the information is accurate. Stark gives a 3.4 percent increase in Christian conversion. From his chart we see a number of 1397 in 50 CE. If we give a mid-fifty CE date for Acts 16:5, then the number of 1397 is low for a church a day movement in Asia Minor. Is the one a day part wrong, or is the population figure wrong? Based on exegesis, I would say the conversion figure is wrong in that it is at least underestimated. It is doubtful that conversion growth is always the same consistent level numerically.

A church a day movement in a region is based on the church being small in size. Imagine multiple, small missional communities in all the cities Paul visits and God multiplying them to one new missional community a day in the time period Luke is summarizing with his panel summary verse in Acts 16:5.

What would some of this look like beyond our exploration in Paul's world? When we are examining ways to connect with people about Jesus Christ:

1. Where is my first connection point with the people I am wishing to reach?

2. Where do general culture and my understanding of this current culture intersect? Where can I meet people best and easiest in light of this?

3. Where can I have the greatest common ground with people that I can reach out to? Common ground is defined as either common interest—hobby, habit, etc. or common place—restaurant, bowling alley, etc.?

4. Where is the lowest hanging fruit? Where has the Lord already prepared the way for me to go and engage people that just might be labeled "easy?"

Notes

[1]Stark, Rodney. *Christianizing the Urban Empire: An Analysis Based on 22 Greco-Roman Cities,* 79; 3000 years of Urban Growth, Chandler and Fox, 303

[2]Longenecker, *John-Acts: The Expositor's Bible Commentary,* 9:431

[3]Claude S. Fischer, "Toward a subcultural theory of urbanism." *American Journal of Sociology* 80:1319-41

[4]Stark, p. 79-80

[5]Stark p. 81

[6]Stark p. 82

[7]Hirsh, *The Forgotten Ways,* p. 18

[8]Stark, *Cities of God,* 76-81

[9]Ibid, 132-34

[10]Ibid, 81-82

[11]Ibid, 94 and 111

[12]Ibid, 116

[13]Ibid, 127

[14]Longenecker, *John-Acts: The Expositor's Bible Commentary,* 9:439

[15]Stark, *Cities of God,* 78

[16]Ibid, 78

[17]Gill, Acts and the Urban Elites, p. 113; contained in David W J Gill and Conrad Gempf Volume 2 - *The book of Acts in its Graeco-Roman setting,* Eerdmans Grand Rapids 1994

[18]Meeks, *First Urban Christians,* 34

[19]Ibid, 17.

[20]Stark, *Cities of God,* 74

[21]Meeks, *First Urban Christians,* 16

[22]Ibid, 17

[23]Ibid, 18

[24]French, Acts and the Roman roads of Asia Minor p. 55 in David W J Gill and Conrad Gempf Volume 2 - *The book of Acts in its Graeco-Roman setting*, Eerdmans Grand Rapids 1994

[25]Ibid, p. 57-58

[26]Meeks, *First Urban Christians*, 9

[27]Stark, *Cities of God*, 60

[28]Meeks, *First Urban Christians*, 14-15

[29]Ibid, p. 15

[30]Longenecker, *John-Acts: The Expositor's Bible Commentary*, 9:438

SECTION 3

MATTERS OF HEALTH

Chapter 8

THE INSURANCE POLICY: KEEPING HEALTHY

*"Worry does not empty tomorrow of its sorrow;
it empties today of its strength."*
Corrie Ten Boom

*"When you gaze long into the abyss,
the abyss also gazes into you."*
Friedrich Nietzsche

*"Are you tired? Worn out? Burned out on religion?
Come to me. Get away with me and you'll recover your life."*
Jesus Christ (*Message,* Matthew 11:28)

Gaze deeply into your own heart, the heart of another, and you will soon see how prevalent burnout is. We are a needy people and while we are in the "work" of helping people like us, how do we keep going?

Keeping Healthy

Our church planting world engages a number of heroes of the faith. We need both those that are full-time on the field planting a church and those that are not full-time in the church planting arena. What we share in this section is applicable to both.

Ministry is hard! You did not have to buy this book to figure that out, with 1,500 ministers leaving vocational ministry each month.[1] We are faced with a strong problem. Those of us in various forms of vocational ministry are potentially sick puppies! We suffer from work and performance addictions, from people-pleasing tendencies—take your pick. Perhaps you are reading this and thinking, "Sorry for the poor slob that faces either of those problems!" But…the man in mirror looks familiar, doesn't he?

We have a real tendency to either bend too far in pleasing people or perhaps bend the other way toward performance addiction problems. Either problem can neutralize our effectiveness. We also have the problem of putting in too much time and the negative impact this has on our families.

Most of us know someone who has "left" vocational ministry because his spouse had had enough. The names are too many to list here (and I would not do it anyway). You are most likely reading this book because you are in vocational ministry of some form—or soon will be. With that in mind, please consider these two ideas of health maintenance.

Five Key Relationships

Common in the church-planting world is the active and intentional dependence on five key relationships.

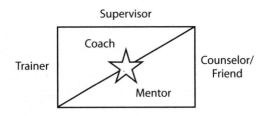

The star in the middle is the church planter. Key to his life are these five relationships.

Five key people in every church planter's life are:

Supervisor: The one who makes the financial decisions of support, the mother church or sending church. This person should carefully understand his role. It is easy to think that church planters are well-balanced individuals who look carefully after their own well-being. There are one or two like this out of 100. Most are built to be so drunk with their vision or passion to plant a church, they let many healthy habits slip or disappear altogether.

The supervisor needs to embrace his role. In this relationship, the supervisor is the one who carries the authority. He needs to have the authority and ability to overrule church-planting and church-planter decisions. This is a hard role, but one we need.

Coach: Coaching is all about skill development. Your coach is the one who is charged with focusing and helping the church planter focus on his skill set and what he needs to fulfill the vision he lives and breathes. The coach and supervisor do well when they can communicate without the coach compromising the confidentiality of the relationship with the planter.

Trainer: A trainer is one that is on-call, based upon need. Perhaps from a coaching session or perhaps from a supervisor's directive, a planter needs to work on a part of his church-planting skill set. The planter may have a clear vision, but is fuzzy on implementation. A trainer can be engaged to assist in implementation.

The planter may need to be more caring in his approach to people. He might be so consumed with his vision and passion that he cannot understand why people are not jumping on board with him. A trainer can come on board to help the planter connect with such issue and figure out an action plan to assist in solving this problem.

Mentor: A mentor is one who focuses most directly on the planter's character development. The mentor needs to be charged with one directive for a church plant: if this new church plant compromises either the planter's health or marital health, then the plug needs to be pulled!

That is a lot of power! But someone must be charged with focus here. As the mentor invests his insight into the life of the planter and his spouse, health is more likely.

Counselor: When a counselor or coach senses or recognizes the need, a planter needs to have a counselor ready. We encourage a planter to have a counselor already chosen and to have met with him at least one time. It is sometimes very hard to "admit" the need for a counselor.

The form of the counselor may change based on many variables, but we all need someone we can talk to and who is very good at listening and giving back key insight.

Jesus' Own Insurance Policy for Our Ministry

I transitioned from a church family that had been my home for 19 years to do what I am doing now. Part of that transition was to obtain new life insurance. I am not as young as I once was. This process, still going on as I write this section of the book, has been insightful. I have had blood work done, an EKG, family history, etc. What I found interesting was how the standards were different on the blood work. Each company had a differing set of values as to what high cholesterol was. For example. I have always been on the borderline of that magic number of 200 or 220 for cholesterol. My number rose to 240 a couple years ago, but has recently come down to 209. I like that. (It has even come down lower.) For some companies, 209 was in the high category; for others, it was not. I like the ones that did not put my cholesterol number in the high part.

Why this story? Health is important and having standards is important. These life insurance companies must pay my family a lot of money if/when I die. They are looking at the risk I pose and how much money they need from me each year to justify paying off my policy. This has motivated them to come up with standards they feel justify the risk they are facing and the reality of the big payoff!

In church planting, there is a big payoff! A new church! Another way to mediate a safer position to personal, spiritual well being while planting or doing any missional activity is to follow Jesus' model.

As I have studied Jesus' ministry approach in the Gospels, one of the greatest tools for doing this study is Gundry and Stanley's *Harmony of the Gospels*. Here are key presuppositions for our study:

Jesus had an intentional three-phase approach to His leadership development:

Phase one was to spend time with people and be a friend to them. Jesus did this during the first year-and-a-half around Jerusalem.[2]

In phase two, Jesus taught those He selected how to share Him and care for others in proactive ministry. He did this after asking them to re-prioritize their time commitments. This occurred during the Great Galilean Ministry, which lasted around one year.[3]

The third phase was when Jesus taught His disciples to multiply. He also, with full intention, taught them how to insure their multiplication and continued work and health at a personal level. In studying this phase of Jesus' ministry, three distinct principles arise, which we will get to later.[4]

Jesus was sent on a mission—John 20:21: "As the Father has sent me, I also send you (NASB)." His mission was clear. He was not only coming to bear the sins of all mankind and die on the cross, shedding His precious blood, but He also was here to imprint His approach to doing a multiplying ministry in His disciples and consequently on us as well. When He completes this process and He sees the fruit of His investment, He celebrates in His own heart like He has not done since arriving (see Luke 10:17-22)! He then gives instruction to assure we carry on the same way He intended. Jesus gives us His insurance policy.

This third phase of Jesus' ministry focuses on three areas. The sections of the Gospels that contain this third phase of His ministry are: Matthew 19:1-20:34; Mark 10:1-10:52; Luke 9:57-19:27; and John 7:10-11:57. Luke gives us more narrative of this multiplication or insurance phase of Jesus' ministry than any of the three gospels.

The three items of focus are:

1. Prayer,
2. Possessions, and
3. Prophecy.

Luke 9 and 10 give a key thought and insight to help us understand what we are working to identify.

John 20:21 – "As the Father has sent me, I also send you." Jesus was sent by His Father with a mission that He faithfully accomplished. We also have to accomplish this same mission. Jesus had one three-year time period in which to make it work. We are not limited by such a time constraint. This is good, and this is bad. Because we think we have time, we run the risk of thinking that we have time. We do not have time. We have much to do.

Luke 9-10 concisely recounts for us what I believe Jesus was doing.

In Luke 9:1-6: Jesus sends out the men that He Himself approached to be with Him—the 12.

In Luke 9:10-11: we have the summary. The 12 returned from a "successful" ministry time and they gave to Him an "accounting" – "exegete" (*diegomai*—to give a detailed and systematic reporting). Then Jesus took them away (*paralambano*) with Him. "Take with" (*paralambano*) is a special word, full of relational meaning regarding leadership development, but more about that later.

This Luke 9 ministry event occurred during Jesus' second phase of ministry (review the three phases of Jesus' ministry). In this accounting, we can imagine that Jesus was quite pleased with the outcome (Mark 6:12-13 for example). But the account in Luke 9 is quite subdued.

But do notice the difference in Luke 10:1-16, which is now part of phase three of Jesus' ministry:

In Luke 10:1-16, Jesus sends out 70 others on the same ministry trip the 12 had been commissioned to make. This is now the third phase of Jesus' multiplication work.

These 70 were those other than the 12. At the very least there were 58 new men here, but I think 70 new men were here. I believe this because of: 1) The ministry direction Jesus was taking—fulfilling His Father's desires; 2) Luke uses (*eteros*) "Other." "Jesus sent 70 *others* out." What this word means is "other of a different kind." In other words, these 70 are/were not part of the original 12 by the use of this word. The word to be used to say they were the same group could be "*allos*" – which means "different of a same group."

Note the differences from this event in comparing Luke 9 and 10:

In Luke 10:17 – they returned with "success."

In Luke 10:18-20 – Satan fell from heaven. This is not history yet (from my perspective). It will be after Revelation 12, but the "human" assurance that Revelation 12 is to occur was this event here in Luke 10. Jesus "proves" that the mission the Father has sent Him on "works!" Satan had no choice but to fall. I am taking this falling as Satan's defeat and then our mimicking of this method assures the fact of Revelation 12 in which Satan literally falls to earth!

In Luke 10:21 – the only place in the Gospels where Jesus is said to be ecstatic in joy! The only place! That has to mean something! Luke tells us that Jesus "rejoiced greatly" in the Holy Spirit (10:21). This is the only Gospel location for such a statement!

Why?

I think it is because Jesus sees that His missional work, the part of His job to ensure this leadership development process continues to work (this would be the first two phases of his ministry) is successful. He can now rest assured that His leadership development and discipleship process is working! And working well. All this then moves Him to the third phase of His ministry, which was to make sure this can multiply in them to others.

Phase three of Jesus' ministry is the insurance layering phase. He has seen great success in the multiplication of disciples and He is thrilled with it. He now moves to the best way to ensure that the process will continue. We see this from Luke's brilliance in composing his gospel.

In order for us to see how Jesus instills the insurance policy of multiplication to the missional work, let us look at Luke 10-22. Luke gives to us more information from this third phase than any of the other three gospels. As we look at this information contained in Luke 10-22, we see a number of interesting points.

We observe that Jesus speaks to three general types of audiences that are named: 1) crowds; 2) Pharisees/Sadducees; 3) Disciples—either named as such or just called "disciples." This is important for us to consider. Our next task is to look at these differing periscopes, or self-contained story sections, and make some observations.

Looking at the list below, note the three general groups Jesus worked with in the last phase of His ministry:

Passage	Addressed to whom	Topic
10:25-37	Lawyer testing Him	Who qualifies as multiplying person
10:38-42	Mary/Martha (disciples)	Priorities/focus
11:1-3	Disciples	Prayer
11:14-54	Crowd/Pharisees	Power/focus
12:1-12	Disciples/crowd	Warnings in truth

12:13-34	Crowd/disciples (13) (22)	Possessions
12:35-53	Crowd/disciples (41)	Jesus' return
12:54-59	Crowd	Recognize times
13:1-9	Crowd	Production
13:10-21	Crowd/synagogue (John 9-10)	Hearing
13:22-30	Crowd	Know saved
13:31-14:24	Pharisees	Focus
14:25-35	Crowd	Discipleship
15:1-32	Pharisees/crowd	Economy of 1
16:1-13	Disciples	Money/possessions
16:14-31	Pharisees	Ears
17:1-10	Disciples (John 11)	Forgiveness/faith
17:11-21	10 lepers	Healing
17:22-37	Disciples	Return of JC
18:1-14	Disciples (Mathew 19, Mark 10)	Prayer
18:15-17	Crowd	Babies
18:18-30	Crowd/ruler	Money
18:31-34	Disciples	Death of JC
18:35-43	Blind man	Healing
19:1-10	Zacchaeus	Focus/priority
19:11-28	"They"	Delay of kingdom *what to do*
19:29-44	Disciples/Pharisees	Triumphal entry
19:45-48	Crowd/disciples	Clean temple
20:1-8	Pharisees	Authority
20:9-19	Crowd	False leaders
20:20-26	Crowd/Pharisees	Focus/Money
20:27-40	Sadducees	Resurr/Interpret.
20:41-44	Sadducees	Focus
20:45-47	Disciples	Focus
21:1-4	Disciples	Money

21:5-36	Disciples	Return of JC
21:37-22:23	Disciples	Communion
22:24-30	Disciples	Greatness
22:31-38	Disciples	Focus/Distress
22:37-46	Disciples (John 13-18) (Betrayal/death/resurrection)	Garden

Let us now take the same list and remove the pericopes (excerpts from larger works) in which Jesus is addressing others, leaving only disciples as the ones to whom He is talking:

Passage	Addressed to whom	Topic
10:38-42	Mary/Martha	Priorities/focus
11:1-13	Disciples	Prayer
12:1-12	Disciples/crowd	Warnings in truth
12:13-34	Crowd/disciples (13) (22)	Possessions
12:35-53	Crowd/disciples (41)	JC return
16:1-13	Disciples	Money/possessions
17:1-10	Disciples	Forgiveness/faith
17:22-37	Disciples	Return of JC
18:1-14	Disciples	Prayer
18:31-34	Disciples	Death of JC
19:1-10	Zacchaeus	Focus/Priority
19:11-28	"They"	Delay of kingdom *what to do*
19:29-44	Disciples/Pharisees	Triumphal entry
19:45-48	Crowd/disciples	Clean temple
20:45-47	Disciples	Focus
21:1-4	Disciples	Money
21:5-36	Disciples	Return of JC
21:37-22:23	Disciples	Communion
22:24-30	Disciples	Greatness
22:31-38	Disciples	Focus/distress
22:37-46	Disciples	Garden

Basic to this line of thinking is the idea that Jesus is going to address differently the differing people He is addressing. He knows clearly what He is planning to do (John 20:21). As we have removed the passages that do not refer to disciples, we see more easily what Jesus focused on in this last phase of His ministry.

As you examine these passages above, you can see that three main categories arise.

Three Major Emphases from Jesus Himself for Multiplication to Continue

I see three major areas of Jesus' teaching at this time.

- Prayer and other specific focus matters—assistance in maintaining re-prioritizing of life.
- Possessions—how to best handle possessions.
- Prophecy—Jesus' return.

Below is one way to categorize the material that Jesus shared with His disciples to instill the insurance policy for multiplication to continue. This is what I have done in selecting these three categories and placing the passages in them.

Prayer and Other Focus Matters

Luke 10:38-42 –Learning to set the "flow" of my life to that which Jesus says is important.

Luke 11:1-13 – How I learn to have powerful prayer impact.

Luke 17:1-10 – "Moving mountains" today! How do I go about doing that?

Luke 18:1-14 – Learning how to battle through prayer all the time; all the way.

Luke 19:1-10 – Learning how to understand life focus and purpose: Why am I here?

Luke 20:45-47 – What things am I careful about?

Luke 22:7-23 - How to build personal confidence with Jesus; how to best connect with Him.

Luke 22:24-30 – Who is truly great?

Luke 22:31-46 – What to do when life falls apart?

Possessions: How to Best Handle Possessions

Luke 12:1-34 – How can I best focus on my possessions and things? What does Jesus have to do with them?

16:1-13 – True eternal perspective on the things of heaven and of earth—all wrapped up in one!

Luke 19:11-28 – We are at war! Heavenly standards!

Luke 19:29-44 – Jesus made an appointment and no one was there.

Luke 21:1-4 – How am I doing based upon this?

Prophecy: Jesus' Soon Return

Luke 12:35-53 - Expectation of Jesus' soon return and how my life shows this. Rating my readiness.

Luke 17:22-37 - The impact of Jesus return – harsh reality.

Luke 21:5-36 - Preparation – am I ready? I have been told.

These three categories are powerful tools to assist in our effort to bring an effective insurance policy to the table to ministry multiplication. How does all this work when we try to apply it to church planting and ensuring health to those engaging in this powerful field of work?

As we train and empower people to plant churches, thinking way beyond the professional clergy, we do well to expose this powerful army of workers to:

Prayer: How they can pray. How we can build a prayer network in the region to give them effective prayer support as they go on their mission.

Possessions: We can teach them how to view material possessions. We can work to lead the way by showing how to be most effective in keeping possessions in their place biblically and missionally. We can use Jesus' teaching and example to elevate mission and value the people we need to reach for Jesus Christ.

Prophecy: Perhaps the most elusive in writing a book because of the incredible diversity of views on Jesus' return. Regardless of one's view of His soon return - we can see from Jesus' own words that He valued His own return and spoke of it in this triplet of exhortation and teaching to place the insurance policy on the new movement He was launching.

Jesus' soon return gives us incredible motivation for our task at hand. Peter summarized it well when he said, "Since all these things are to be destroyed in this way, what sort of people ought you to be in holy conduct and godliness, looking for and hastening the coming of the day of God, because of which the heavens will be destroyed by burning, and the elements will melt with intense heat!" (2 Peter 3:11-12 NASB)

It is staggering to think that Jesus has set up this world so that I can hasten His return! Imagine that! I am able to do that by engaging my calling and using my gifting! What a gift!

Notes

[1]Kinnamen and Ells, *Leaders That Last,* 10

[2]Robert L. Thomas and Stanley N. Gundry, editors, *A Harmony of the Gospels* (Chicago: Moody Press, 1978, fourth printing 1981) 36-46

[3]Ibid, 47-129

[4]Ibid, 130-179

Chapter 9

SUSTAINABILITY IN LIGHT OF EXPECTATIONS

"God is a comedian playing to an audience too afraid to laugh."
Voltaire

"We didn't lose the game; we just ran out of time."
Vince Lombardi

". . . using every adversity to stimulate you to creative survival, to concentrate your attention on the bare essentials, so you'll live, really live, and not complacently just get by on good behavior."
Jesus Christ (Luke 16:8b-9 *Message*)

In the first church plant in which I was involved, from a mother church perspective, I learned how powerful expectations are. Our church daughtered for the first time in 1997 and the new church began very well. The planter was a (then) young single man who did a great job. He formed the group well, and he led them in their development. We hived off some of our mother church family. It began well. But, there eventually arose challenges, as in all church plants!

The greatest tragedy of the plant had to do with my inadequacies. I was not well enough versed in the realities of church planting at this phase of my life and ministry to curb what was about to happen. It was the late nineties. Though the church planter was doing a great job and leading in a missional way, because his group did not attain a certain size, he and his team became quite discouraged and I was unable to convince him of his "success." He and his team were very successful, both numerically and through mission.

There were expectations the group did not meet. Where did these expectations come from? They came from our church culture, they came from many different places. These expectations had a significant role in defeating that church plant. We brought the group back to the mother church with the goal of re-launching them in a couple years, but we never did.

As I have mulled this over through the years, the role of expectations has haunted me. They appear all powerful. They are not, but they do have considerable powers. As I plant a church, and I do not meet expectations, I am a failure – at least in my own eyes; and unfortunately, often in the eyes of others.

If I remain missional in my church and carry forth the necessary systems to preach the gospel to people and meet them in a relevant way, how successful am I? In the GSE church planting process, expectations are confronted immediately. As a matter of fact, expectations can become a real asset. In this process, with the use of "nonprofessional" workers, or emphasis on the priesthood of the believer, we are able to manage our expectations in a righteous way. Since we are not investing large amounts of money, we are able to allow people to use their spiritual gifts in reaching people in the harvest with greater allowances for time.

That we focus on small churches with moderate growth is a significant key. Our expectations can meet God's reality better this way. Most church planting treatises are written from the large church situation. "Ninety-five percent of the literature on church growth and health should concentrate on healthy, small churches that can multiply and give birth to other small churches."[1] Unfortunately, this is not the case.

Upon what foundation should we place our expectations? We need to have expectations and we need not fear high accountability and hard questions. Unfortunately, we gravitate toward nickels and noses. Nickels and noses are important. Noses are people. But what if we mold expectations around systems that place their highest focus on missional work, on planted churches that are sharing the gospel, actively producing healthy disciples who are reproducing themselves in others? Those are good "noses!" We might shy away from nickels and noses, and allow the Lord to form our expectations around His mission.

We are after vision realization. But how do we get there? If I desire to be sodalic in thinking and action, then I must come to grips with a certain truth that touches expectations: the vision itself is the far more important issue than even my own survival.[2] Change like that is hard and cuts very deeply. How can I mold my expectations to such a vision as this? Expecting great things from God is good. He can deliver. May this expectation of God mold me to risk great things for God.

Ways to Battle Expectations and/or Ways to Understand Biblical Success

Stetzer and Bird report, "The likelihood of survivability increased by over 400 percent when the church planter has a 'realistic' understanding and expectations of the church planting experience." They go on to say, "But all planters must tie their expectations to who they are and where they plant. They must base their expectations in the tangible world of their own skills, the limitations inherent in their church model, and the demographic probabilities of their community."[3] This is good advice. Other thoughts we can contribute to this conversation are these:

I need to have a clear understanding of the missional effort with clear conversations about the likely beginning goal and presenting problems.

> If a church multiplication movement is to happen in the United States, it is highly unlikely to come from our current structures and systems, and not even from our more vigorous approaches to church planting in recent years. If we carry our current methods and approaches to their logical end, maybe we could push the current system harder to generate a few more churches, but it is already close to capacity. We already have almost all the church planting that our current money can buy and our current systems can support.[4]

I agree with Stetzer and Bird — we are at capacity based on a financial evaluation, especially in our current economy. As our economy may or may not improve, lessons we are learning need to tell us not to plan on large financial foundations for church multiplication.

Our need is to begin with the end in mind. If we wish to see 33 robustly healthy churches per 10,000 people in North America, then we must see our definition of success change and leave the large church desire of our current time in its own context.

How would this situation work itself out? If a community is 3,000 in size (I am using smaller numbers for easier math), we would want to see 10 new robustly healthy churches there who are aggressively evangelistic and multiplying themselves in their discipleship. The job of the 10 robustly healthy churches is to each focus on 300 people in the town of 3,000.

A Significant Problem

What is a big problem with this idea? NIMBY. Have you ever met NIMBY? He is alive and well! Mr. NIMBY is "not-in-my-backyard." NIMBY is perhaps our biggest problem as we imagine a true multiplication movement in the U.S. So many of us suffer from this disease. As long I can just grow my own church or see to it that this effort benefits my own church world, it is okay. But when another church comes to my backyard and keeps me from gaining a family or so, then it is not okay.

NIMBY can be what is behind the need to give "permission" to a project to begin in my own backyard or even someone else's. NIMBY may be behind the thought that there are enough churches already in my area, and we do not need any more.

But here is the reality as expressed by multiple authors addressing the shape of the church in the USA:

Brian McNichol shares that when a church is:

- 0-3 years old: This church averages 10 people won to Christ per 100 members;
- 3-15 years old: This church averages five people won to Christ per 100 members;

- 15+ years old: This church averages three people won to Christ per 100 members.[5]

America is becoming increasingly unchurched:

- 1900: There were 28 churches per 10,000 Americans;
- 1950: There were 17 churches per 10,000 Americans;
- 2000: There were 12 churches per 10,000 Americans.[6]

Bill Easum reports: There are now nearly 60 percent fewer churches per 10,000 persons than in 1920.[7]

According to Hugh Halter:

- 1910 – 25 percent of people in America unchurched;
- 1990 – 65 percent of people in America unchurched;
- 2000 – 75 percent of people in America unchurched;
- 2025 – 90-95 percent of people in America are unchurched (projected).[8]

Tom Nebel:

- 4,000 churches a year close doors annually. U.S.—2002; now 4,000 new churches planted;
- Lose 2.7 million from church each year;
- U.S.: third largest mission field today;
- Only continent except for Europe in which Christianity is not growing;
- No county in the U.S. grew even 1 percent in attendance in the last 10 years—2002; in 2008, one county in Hawaii grew![9]

Question: What is 50,000 miles long, reaches around the world two times, and grows longer by more than a mile each day?

Answer: The line of people in the United States currently untouched by your church and mine.[10]

Regardless of how you might feel about NIMBY, there is a need for another church near you to help fulfill the Great Commission. NIMBY is a pandemic issue in the West. Perhaps it is in the East as well. How can we address this matter?

Let us consider this:

Invest some time evaluating how connected to NIMBY I might

be. Self-diagnosis is a powerful ally when dealing with such a pandemic problem.

- How open am I to engage another church plant in my own facility?
- How open am I to planting a church right next door to me with us giving them the land upon which to erect a building?
- How willing am I to hive off 10+ percent of my church family to a new church plant in my own vicinity?
- To what extent am I held captive by the historic practices of my church family (not denominationally driven) when it comes to investing in the harvest?
- How secure is my job in my current church if a new church were planted next door?

From these questions we find ways to expose our own deep issues and vulnerabilities. This is a good exercise for us—for me. All of God's promises to meet our needs and provide are as true now as the last time He met our needs.

Invest time exploring relational ways to enter into safe conversations about NIMBY. What I mean is this: One reason NIMBY lives so powerfully in our hearts is because it lives next and near to a common core identity we have. When I have as my core identity some form of ministry, then I can be offended or angered to a core level by someone challenging me through NIMBY.

When that challenge comes, it is so powerful because it is so tied to who I view myself to be. As a situation challenges the main essence of how I see myself and how I live my life, I am going to work hard to keep that identity going—even though that identity may not be/ is not biblical at all.

The core identity that I must have is the one so powerfully expressed in Matthew 3:13-4:4:

> "Then Jesus arrived from Galilee at the Jordan coming to John, to be baptized by him. But John tried to prevent Him, saying, 'I have need to be baptized by You, and do You come to me?' But Jesus answering said to him, 'Permit it at this time; for in this way it is fitting for us to fulfill all righteousness.' Then he permitted Him. After being baptized, Jesus

came up immediately from the water; and behold, the heavens were opened, and he saw the Spirit of God descending as a dove and lighting on Him, and behold, a voice out of the heavens said, 'This is My beloved Son, in whom I am well-pleased.' Then Jesus was led up by the Spirit into the wilderness to be tempted by the devil. And after He had fasted forty days and forty nights, He then became hungry. And the tempter came and said to Him, 'If You are the Son of God, command that these stones become bread.' But He answered and said, 'It is written, *"Man shall not live on bread alone, but on every word that proceeds out of the mouth of God* (NASB)."'"

In this passage we see that Jesus is baptized to formally begin His public ministry. As the passage indicates, the Father expresses to His own son the main message He needed to hear and knew to be true and affirmed by the most important person in His life. This is how Jesus begins the formal, public part of his ministry. That core level, basic information dealt with Jesus' core identity: He is His Father's beloved son!

It is no coincidence that the first effort at significant identity theft is recorded in Matthew 4:1-4. Satan attacks first what he knows God values most—core identity. Core identity is what Satan loves to attack the most.

When the enemy has convinced me that my core identity is tied to my church or to being a pastor and has moved me from where I should be to this place, then NIMBY is powerful! They would work as core, evil twins.

The core identity that I need to have is well expressed that I am God's beloved one! There is nothing more beautiful nor more necessary than this. It is true for me and true for anyone who has received Jesus Christ as his/her savior.

John shares more with us on this matter of core identity in 1 John 2:28-3:3:

"Now, little children, abide in Him, so that when He appears, we may have confidence and not shrink away from Him in shame at His coming. If you know that He is righteous, you know that everyone also who practices righteousness is born of Him. See how great a love the Father has bestowed on us, that we would be called children of God; and such we are. For this reason the world does not know us, because it did not know Him. Beloved, now we are children of God, and it has not appeared as yet what we will be. We know that when He appears, we will be like Him, because we will see Him just as He is. And everyone who has this hope fixed on Him purifies himself, just as He is pure (NASB)."

John also clarifies for us that central to our core is the truth that I am God's beloved son! John so powerfully places our core identity at the center of how we proceed through life:

"Beloved, now we are children of God, and it has not appeared as yet what we will be. We know that when He appears, we will be like Him, because we will see Him just as He is. And everyone who has this hope fixed on Him purifies himself, just as He is pure (NASB)."

This focus is key for us when it comes to managing and destroying NIMBY (among so many other things). NIMBY can strike such fear and concern deep within our own hearts. The overriding message of Scripture is that regardless of where I am in my time here on earth, Jesus can come at any time and tell me that everything is OK.

There is an overwhelming set of examples in Scripture that show us how much God cares for us at this level. There are many examples of God connecting with "me" and letting me know that all is OK because of His intense love for me because I am His beloved son/daughter!

Consider these examples:

Example 1: Genesis 15:1-23: "After these things the word of the LORD came to Abram in a vision, saying,

'Do not fear, Abram,
I am a shield to you;
Your reward shall be very great.' Abram said, 'O Lord GOD,

what will You give me, since I am childless, and the heir of my house is Eliezer of Damascus?' And Abram said, 'Since You have given no offspring to me, one born in my house is my heir.' Then behold, the word of the LORD came to him, saying, 'This man will not be your heir; but one who will come forth from your own body, he shall be your heir.' And He took him outside and said, 'Now look toward the heavens, and count the stars, if you are able to count them.' And He said to him, 'So shall your descendants be.' Then he believed in the LORD; and He reckoned it to him as righteousness. And He said to him, 'I am the LORD who brought you out of Ur of the Chaldeans, to give you this land to possess it.' He said, 'O Lord GOD, how may I know that I will possess it?' So He said to him, 'Bring Me a three year old heifer, and a three year old female goat, and a three year old ram, and a turtledove, and a young pigeon.' Then he brought all these to Him and cut them in two, and laid each half opposite the other; but he did not cut the birds. The birds of prey came down upon the carcasses, and Abram drove them away. Now when the sun was going down, a deep sleep fell upon Abram; and behold, terror and great darkness fell upon him. God said to Abram, 'Know for certain that your descendants will be strangers in a land that is not theirs, where they will be enslaved and oppressed four hundred years. But I will also judge the nation whom they will serve, and afterward they will come out with many possessions. As for you, you shall go to your fathers in peace; you will be buried at a good old age. Then in the fourth generation they will return here, for the iniquity of the Amorite is not yet complete.' It came about when the sun had set, that it was very dark, and behold, there appeared a smoking oven and a flaming torch, which passed between these pieces. On that day the LORD made a covenant with Abram, saying 'To your descendants I have given this land, from the river of Egypt as far as the great river, the river Euphrates: the

Kenite and the Kenizzite and the Kadmonite and the Hittite
and the Perizzite and the Rephaimand the Amorite and the
Canaanite and the Girgashite and the Jebusite (NASB).'"

Presenting problem to Abram: You said I would have an heir
(Genesis 12). Is he Eliezar?

God's presence: God's presence made clear to Abram and even on
the alarming side in vss. 20ff.

God's solution: It will be OK. But God did not solve the matter
at this time in the passage.

Example 2: Genesis 32:22-32: "Now he arose that same night and
took his two wives and his two maids and his eleven children, and
crossed the ford of the Jabbok. He took them and sent them across
the stream. And he sent across whatever he had."

Then Jacob was left alone, and a man wrestled with him until
daybreak. When he saw that he had not prevailed against him, he
touched the socket of his thigh; so the socket of Jacob's thigh was
dislocated while he wrestled with him. Then he said, 'Let me go, for
the dawn is breaking.' But he said, 'I will not let you go unless you
bless me.' So he said to him, 'What is your name?' And he said, 'Jacob.' He said, 'Your name shall no longer be Jacob, but Israel; for you
have striven with God and with men and have prevailed.' Then Jacob
asked him and said, 'Please tell me your name.' But he said, 'Why is
it that you ask my name?' And he blessed him there. So Jacob named
the place Peniel, for *he said,* 'I have seen God face to face, yet my life
has been preserved.' Now the sun rose upon him just as he crossed
over Penuel, and he was limping on his thigh. Therefore, to this day
the sons of Israel do not eat the sinew of the hip, which is on the
socket of the thigh, because he touched the socket of Jacob's thigh in
the sinew of the hip."

Presenting problem: Esau is coming with 400 men! (Genesis
32:6). Jacob is scared to death. He begins petitioning God and reminding God about their "deal." "God, you said you would bless
me!" (Genesis 32:9 ff.)

God's presence: Jesus wrestles with Jacob through the night and
then touches his hip and subdues him. I personally believe Jesus

could have "taken" Jacob any time during the night, He did not because this was for Jacob's sake, not Jesus' sake.

God's solution: It will be OK. I bless you. God did not solve the problem of Esau but made Jacob face it!

Example 3: Exodus 3:1-22: "Now Moses was pasturing the flock of Jethro his father-in-law, the priest of Midian; and he led the flock to the west side of the wilderness and came to Horeb, the mountain of God. The angel of the LORD appeared to him in a blazing fire from the midst of a bush; and he looked, and behold, the bush was burning with fire, yet the bush was not consumed. So Moses said, 'I must turn aside now and see this marvelous sight, why the bush is not burned up.' When the LORD saw that he turned aside to look, God called to him from the midst of the bush and said, 'Moses, Moses!' And he said, 'Here I am.' Then He said, 'Do not come near here; remove your sandals from your feet, for the place on which you are standing is holy ground.' He said also, 'I am the God of your father, the God of Abraham, the God of Isaac, and the God of Jacob.' Then Moses hid his face, for he was afraid to look at God.

The LORD said, 'I have surely seen the affliction of My people who are in Egypt, and have given heed to their cry because of their taskmasters, for I am aware of their sufferings. So I have come down to deliver them from the power of the Egyptians, and to bring them up from that land to a good and spacious land, to a land flowing with milk and honey, to the place of the Canaanite and the Hittite and the Amorite and the Perizzite and the Hivite and the Jebusite. Now, behold, the cry of the sons of Israel has come to Me; furthermore, I have seen the oppression with which the Egyptians are oppressing them.

Therefore, come now, and I will send you to Pharaoh, so that you may bring My people, the sons of Israel, out of Egypt.' But Moses said to God, 'Who am I, that I should go to Pharaoh, and that I should bring the sons of Israel out of Egypt?' And He said, 'Certainly I will be with you, and this shall be the sign to you that it is I who have sent you: when you have brought the people out of Egypt, you shall worship God at this mountain.'

Then Moses said to God, 'Behold, I am going to the sons of Israel, and I will say to them, "The God of your fathers has sent me to you." Now they may say to me, "What is His name?" What shall I say to them?' God said to Moses, 'I AM WHO I AM'; and He said, 'Thus you shall say to the sons of Israel, I AM has sent me to you.' God, furthermore, said to Moses, 'Thus you shall say to the sons of Israel, "The LORD, the God of your fathers, the God of Abraham, the God of Isaac, and the God of Jacob, has sent me to you." This is My name forever, and this is My memorial-name to all generations.' 'Go and gather the elders of Israel together and say to them, "The LORD, the God of your fathers, the God of Abraham, Isaac and Jacob, has appeared to me, saying, "I am indeed concerned about you and what has been done to you in Egypt. "So I said, I will bring you up out of the affliction of Egypt to the land of the Canaanite and the Hittite and the Amorite and the Perizzite and the Hivite and the Jebusite, to a land flowing with milk and honey."' "They will pay heed to what you say; and you with the elders of Israel will come to the king of Egypt and you will say to him, 'The LORD, the God of the Hebrews, has met with us. So now, please, let us go a three days' journey into the wilderness, that we may sacrifice to the LORD our God.' "But I know that the king of Egypt will not permit you to go, except under compulsion. "So I will stretch out My hand and strike Egypt with all My miracles which I shall do in the midst of it; and after that he will let you go. "I will grant this people favor in the sight of the Egyptians; and it shall be that when you go, you will not go empty-handed. "But every woman shall ask of her neighbor and the woman who lives in her house, articles of silver and articles of gold, and clothing; and you will put them on your sons and daughters. Thus you will plunder the Egyptians (NASB)."

Presenting problem: Moses has fled Egypt because he has killed a man. He is a murderer. He is working for his father-in-law and God meets him. The presenting problem(s) are many, but suffice it to say that God is dealing with a beloved son who is in need of His grace and love and affirmation so as to be empowered for mission.

God's presence: Burning bush that is not consumed.

God's solution: God does not solve any of Moses' problems. He simply shows him the job before him and empowers him to do it. He gives to Moses what Moses needed to carry on the job. Moses is still a murderer and still wondering and fleeing at this time.

Example 4: Exodus 33:12-23: "Then Moses said to the LORD, 'See, You say to me, "Bring up this people!" But You Yourself have not let me know whom You will send with me. Moreover, You have said, "I have known you by name, and you have also found favor in My sight." Now therefore, I pray You, if I have found favor in Your sight, let me know Your ways that I may know You, so that I may find favor in Your sight. Consider too, that this nation is Your people.' And He said, 'My presence shall go *with you,* and I will give you rest.' Then he said to Him, 'If Your presence does not go *with us,* do not lead us up from here. For how then can it be known that I have found favor in Your sight, I and Your people? Is it not by Your going with us, so that we, I and Your people, may be distinguished from all the *other* people who are upon the face of the earth?'

The LORD said to Moses, 'I will also do this thing of which you have spoken; for you have found favor in My sight and I have known you by name.' Then Moses said, 'I pray You, show me Your glory!' And He said, 'I Myself will make all My goodness pass before you, and will proclaim the name of the LORD before you; and I will be gracious to whom I will be gracious, and will show compassion on whom I will show compassion.' But He said, 'You cannot see My face, for no man can see Me and live!' Then the LORD said, 'Behold, there is a place by Me, and you shall stand *there* on the rock; and it will come about, while My glory is passing by, that I will put you in the cleft of the rock and cover you with My hand until I have passed by. Then I will take My hand away and you shall see My back, but My face shall not be seen (NASB).'"

Presenting problem: Golden calf, rebellious people, sexual immortality, and movement away from God.

God's presence: Moses desperately needs something in order to move on. He needs God to meet him and let him know that all is well, that God is going to do as He said. God does so.

God's solution: He gives Moses exactly what he needs, but He does not solve the problem of the calf and the rebellion, He simply tells Moses and shows Moses what Moses needed to go on.

Example 5: Joshua 5:13-15: "Now it came about when Joshua was by Jericho, that he lifted up his eyes and looked, and behold, a man was standing opposite him with his sword drawn in his hand, and Joshua went to him and said to him, 'Are you for us or for our adversaries?' He said, 'No; rather I indeed come now *as* captain of the host of the LORD.' And Joshua fell on his face to the earth, and bowed down, and said to him, 'What has my lord to say to his servant?' The captain of the LORD'S host said to Joshua, 'Remove your sandals from your feet, for the place where you are standing is holy.' And Joshua did so."

Presenting problem: Moving ahead after crossing the Jordan river. In Joshua 5:1-12, Joshua has the males circumcised. They observed the Passover and ate produce of the land and the manna stopped coming. Now what is next for Joshua?

God's presence: Joshua, just outside Jericho, looks up and there is Jesus. Joshua asks a question that I think is an acceptable question: "Are you for us or for our adversaries?" (Joshua 5:13). Jesus answers powerfully: "No."

God's solution: Joshua is thinking in the wrong direction. In order for him to move on as God's beloved son he needs to do this: "Take off your shoes." There is no solution to anything except Joshua meets Jesus at a key time necessary for movement forward.

Example 6: Revelation 1:9-20: "I, John, your brother and fellow partaker in the tribulation and kingdom and perseverance which are in Jesus, was on the island called Patmos because of the word of God and the testimony of Jesus. I was in the Spirit on the Lord's day, and I heard behind me a loud voice like *the sound* of a trumpet, saying, 'Write in a book what you see, and send *it* to the seven churches: to Ephesus and to Smyrna and to Pergamum and to Thyatira and to Sardis and to Philadelphia and to Laodicea.'

Then I turned to see the voice that was speaking with me. And having turned I saw seven golden lampstands; and in the middle of the lampstands *I saw* one like a son of man, clothed in a robe reaching to the feet, and girded across His chest with a golden sash. His head and His hair were white like white wool, like snow; and His eyes were like a flame of fire. His feet *were* like burnished bronze, when it has been made to glow in a furnace, and His voice *was* like the sound of many waters. In His right hand He held seven stars, and out of His mouth came a sharp two-edged sword; and His face was like the sun shining in its strength.

When I saw Him, I fell at His feet like a dead man. And He placed His right hand on me, saying, 'Do not be afraid; I am the first and the last, and the living One; and I was dead, and behold, I am alive forevermore, and I have the keys of death and of Hades. Therefore write the things, which you have seen, and the things, which are, and the things, which will take place after these things. As for the mystery of the seven stars which you saw in My right hand, and the seven golden lampstands: the seven stars are the angels of the seven churches, and the seven lampstands are the seven churches.'"

Presenting problem: John is at the prison island Patmos because of the testimony of Jesus Christ and the Word of God. John is in prison.

God's presence: John meets Jesus after many years of not seeing each other! John responds in what I believe to be the biblical way—falling to the ground as a dead man.

God's solution: Please note what happens next: Jesus empties His hands of the "seven stars" (Rev 1:16) so that He can touch John with His right hand and say, "Do not be afraid..."

Jesus says it will be OK. I am here to let you know that. What a message to get—what a touch to get when you need it! Jesus does not solve John's Patmos problem, but He does tell him it is okay and I am with you!

There are many other examples: Gideon in Judges 6; Isaiah in Isaiah 6; Ezekiel in Ezekiel 1; Daniel in Daniel 7 and 10, just to name a few. In each case the presenting problem was not "solved" but God showed up and affirmed in His dear servant his core identity: You are my beloved son, it is going to be all right!

My core identity is key to fighting NIMBY (Not In My Back-yard). As I am comfortable and content in who I am in Jesus, then I can more easily fight the fear of someone else coming into my territory and working in the harvest near me.

NIMBY also influences how I, as a pastor, view the rest of my church family. This application of NIMBY also makes me not willing to have my church family engage in matters outside my own church family. If and when this is true it means I will not be open to having the "laity" engage in efforts that do not benefit my own church family.

The truth is that helping my own church family engage a church-planting effort does help my own congregation. It helps me become more kingdom centered and blessed. For there to be 10 robustly healthy churches in a small area like a town of 3,000 or a part of a larger area focusing in on a segment of 3,000, we would need to see NIMBY cared for. Perhaps we can see this as we engage greater laity involvement. Money is then not as important as for paid clergy involvement.

I need to have a clear understanding of biblical success

Skill set and heart - these are two powerful foundations for helping us focus on biblical success. From the heart perspective, we can focus on these heart related matters:

Heart

Suffering

This is not a popular topic but one fit for the heart. Jesus calls us to engage this concept and apply it deeply into our hearts. Often, at least to me, suffering in church planting is that I may not make much money or even any money. That is often the case—always has been and most likely always will be.

Of all the church planters I know, they would gladly give up or live with the lack of money if they could trade some other aspect of suffering they are having to endure. A planter would gladly live with the lack of money issues to not have to live with the Satanic push-back on his extended family or if he could avoid the Satanic attack on his immediate family, or even the extra high discouragement that sets in so quickly that for some reason was not present in the established church environment.

Am I saying that pastoring in an established church environment is easier or less attacked? No. The more likely explanation is that it is all perception. The reality can be that in the established church there is a much better prayer networking that is keeping some of these Satanic things away. But in the planter environment, often "out of sight" is "out of mind." And the prayer support can wane and the Satanic pushback can be extreme.

Though always present, the ease with which I can move from healthy thinking to abject self-rejection is amazing. It is my easiest example of knowing what "warp drive" speed is all about, a la *Star Trek*. In my planting experience, self rejection of the significance and importance of the church planting mission so easily surfaces.

With this as an example, let us look at the Scriptures to form and mold our expectations on such things:

1 Peter 1:6-9 "In this you greatly rejoice, even though now for a little while, if necessary, you have been distressed by various trials, so that the proof of your faith, being more precious than gold which is perishable, even though tested by fire, may be found to result in praise and glory and honor at the revelation of Jesus Christ; and though you have not seen Him, you love Him, and though you do not see Him now, but believe in Him, you greatly rejoice with joy inexpressible and full of glory, obtaining as the outcome of your faith the salvation of your souls (NASB)."

1 Peter 2:18-25 "Servants, be submissive to your masters with all respect, not only to those who are good and gentle, but also to those who are unreasonable. For this finds favor, if for the sake of conscience toward God a person bears up under sorrows when suffering unjustly. For what credit is there if, when you sin and are harshly treated, you endure it with patience? But if when you do what is right and suffer for it you patiently endure it, this finds favor with God. For you have been called for this purpose, since Christ also suffered for you, leaving you can example for you to follow in His steps, who committed no sin, nor was any deceit found in His mouth; and while being reviled, He did not revile in return; while suffering, He uttered no threats, but kept entrusting Himself to Him who judges righteously; and He Himself bore our sins in His body on the cross, so that we might die to sin and live to righteousness; for by His wounds you were healed. For you were continually straying like sheep, but now you have returned to the Shepherd and Guardian of your soul (NASB)."

1 Peter 3:13-17 "Who is there to harm you if you prove zealous for what is good? But even if you should suffer for the sake of righteousness, you are blessed. And do not fear their intimidation, and do not be troubled, but sanctify Christ as Lord in your hearts, always being ready to make a defense to everyone who asks you to give an account for the hope that is in you, yet with gentleness and reverence; and keep a good conscience so that in the thing in which you are slandered, those who revile your good behavior in Christ will be put to shame. For it is better, if God should will it so, that you suffer for doing what is right rather than for doing what is wrong (NASB)."

1 Peter 4:1-6 "Therefore, since Christ has suffered in the flesh, arm yourselves also with the same purpose, because he who has suffered in the flesh has ceased from sin, so as to live the rest of the time in the flesh no longer for the lusts of men, but for the will of God. For the time already past is sufficient for you to have carried out the desire of the Gentiles, having pursued a course of sensuality, lusts, drunkenness, carousing, drinking parties and abominable idolatries. In all this, they are surprised that you do not run with them into the same excesses of dissipation, and they malign you; but they will give account to Him who is ready to judge the living and the dead. For the gospel has for this purpose been preached even to those who are dead, that though they are judged in the flesh as men, they may live in the spirit according to the will of God (NASB)."

Romans 8:18-27 "For I consider that the sufferings of this present time are not worthy to be compared with the glory that is to be revealed to us. For the anxious longing of the creation waits eagerly for the revealing of the sons of God. For the creation was subjected to futility, not willingly, but because of Him who subjected it, in hope that the creation itself also will be set free from its slavery to corruption into the freedom of the glory of the children of God. For we know that the whole creation groans and suffers the pains of childbirth together until now. And not only this, but also we ourselves, having the first fruits of the Spirit, even we ourselves groan within ourselves, waiting eagerly for our adoption as sons, the redemption of our body. For in hope we have been saved, but hope that is seen is not hope; for who hopes for what he already sees? But if we hope for what we do not see, with perseverance we wait eagerly for it. In the same way the Spirit also helps our weakness; for awe do not know how to pray as we should, but the Spirit Himself intercedes for us with groanings too deep for words; and He who searches the hearts knows what the mind of the Spirit is, because He intercedes for the saints according to the will of God (NASB)."

Phil. 1:27-30 "Only conduct yourselves in a manner worthy of the gospel of Christ, so that whether I come and see you or remain absent, I will hear of you that you are standing firm in done spirit, with one mind striving together for the faith of the gospel; in no way alarmed by your opponents — which is a sign of destruction for them, but of salvation for you, and that too, from God. For to you it has been granted for Christ's sake, not only to believe in Him, but also to suffer for His sake, experiencing the same conflict which you saw in me, and now hear to be in me (NASB)."

Phil. 3:8-10 "But whatever things were gain to me, those things I have counted as loss for the sake of Christ. More than that, I count all things to be loss in view of the surpassing value of knowing Christ Jesus my Lord, for whom I have suffered the loss of all things, and count them but rubbish so that I may gain Christ, and may be found in Him, not having a righteousness of my own derived from the Law, but that which is through faith in Christ, the righteousness which comes from God on the basis of faith, that I may know Him and the power of His resurrection and the fellowship of His sufferings, being conformed to His death; in order that I may attain to the resurrection from the dead (NASB)."

2 Tim. 1:8-18 "Therefore do not be ashamed of the testimony of our Lord or of me His prisoner, but join with me in suffering for the gospel according to the power of God, who has saved us and called us with a holy calling, not according to our works, but according to His own purpose and grace which was granted us in Christ Jesus from all eternity, but now has been revealed by the appearing of our Savior Christ Jesus, who abolished death and brought life and immortality to light through the gospel, for which I was appointed a preacher and an apostle and a teacher. For this reason I also suffer these things, but I am not ashamed; for I know whom I have believed and I am convinced that He is able to guard what I have entrusted to Him until that day. Retain the standard of sound words, which you have heard from me, in the faith and love, which are in Christ Jesus. Guard, through the Holy Spirit who dwells in us, the treasure, which has been entrusted to you. You are aware of the fact that all who are in Asia turned away from me, among whom are Phygelus and Hermogenes. The Lord grant mercy to the house of Onesiphorus, for he often refreshed me and was not ashamed of my chains; but when he was in Rome, he eagerly searched for me and found me — the Lord grant to him to find mercy from the Lord on that day — and you know very well what services he rendered at Ephesus (NASB)."

James 5:8-11 "You too be patient; strengthen your hearts, for the coming of the Lord is near. Do not complain, brethren, against one another, so that you yourselves may not be judged; behold, the Judge is standing right at the door. As an example, brethren, of suffering and patience, take the prophets who spoke in the name of the Lord. We count those blessed who endured. You have heard of the endurance of Job and have seen the outcome of the Lord's dealings, that the Lord is full of compassion and is merciful (NASB)."

Engagement of the Laity (Priesthood of the Believer)

I think it is safe to say that we all believe in the "priesthood of the believer." We all—to varying degrees—work hard at equipping our church family and having them engage ministry of all kinds. I think we would all agree that our "success" in ministry is based on how we can assist others to engage in ministry and to see them use their gifting to do amazing things for Jesus Christ.

What if Jesus used the criteria for "biblical success" as this: How many non- professional clergy are we able to equip and insert into ministry efforts like church planting? Church planting in the West has a definite flavor of "professional" tied to it. How refreshing it would be to have the flavor of "layman" tied to it. What if laymen were planting 60 percent of the new churches in North America?

1 Peter 2:4-5: "And coming to Him as to a living stone which has been rejected by men, but is choice and precious in the sight of

God, you also, as living stones, are being built up as a spiritual house for a holy priesthood, to offer up spiritual sacrifices acceptable to God through Jesus Christ (NASB)."

Revelation 1:4-6: "John to the seven churches that are in Asia: Grace to you and peace, from Him who is and who was and who is to come, and from the seven Spirits who are before His throne, and from Jesus Christ, the faithful witness, the firstborn of the dead, and the ruler of the kings of the earth. To Him who loves us and released us from our sins by His blood—and He has made us to be a kingdom, priests to His God and Father—to Him be the glory and the dominion forever and ever. Amen (NASB)."

Abundance Mindset

As we do ministry we can have any combination of options. We can see an abundance of resources on the ministry platform, or we can develop a scarcity mindset. A scarcity mindset is when I do not see adequate resources available to accomplish ministry as I wish.

Many think that if we have enough money or people we can accomplish anything. And it is because we do not have enough money or people that we do not accomplish our goal in ministry.

Biblical reality hits us hard that God has given us all the resources we need to make this all happen. In what ways?

- Has God given us enough vision?

- Has God given us enough people?

- Has God given us enough relationships?

- Has God given us enough understanding to know what this journey is like?

- Has God given us enough physical resources to carry out the job?

I would say yes to all of them. Though we may live in a day in which the established church's financial investment is less than it once was, we still live in a day when the financial resources are available for new ways of planting or new ways of engaging the planting of new churches.

Allowance/Acceptance of Small/Smaller church

If I have a choice, which one would I rather focus on? Millions of new churches or one large church?

Stetzer and Bird share on this matter:

> Our caution about big churches is that the more they grow, the more likely they are to grow by addition rather than multiplication. It is never easy to give up the people and resources necessary to multiply. The larger a church becomes the greater the temptation becomes to take on a sedentary position to movemental Christianity. The larger the church, the less able it is to multiply itself—unless its leaders continually make heroes of small replicable groups, teams, or classes. In reality, a church grows bigger by doing small better.[11]

Passion

Passion is key to any endeavor we take on for Jesus Christ. The passion passage most often used to illustrate this concept is Ephesians 3:20-21:

> "Now to Him who is able to do far more abundantly beyond all that we ask or think, according to the power that works within us, to Him be the glory in the church and in Christ Jesus to all generations forever and ever. Amen. (NASB)"

A common response is, "I can ask and think of a lot!" I am quite sure God is completely fine with that response. We are most likely the ones who are not fine with God's response back: "Then deny yourself and take up your cross and follow me; I need you to hate your mom, dad, sister, brother, husband, wife, child, and even yourself to be my disciple." (Luke 14)

As God responds with such words we might then begin to think less about "a lot" of things. So, the problem is not God, but me, as usual.

But how can I more easily arrive at "seeing" Ephesians 3:20-21 in my life? I think the answer lies in what Paul prayed in Ephesians 3:14-19.

Paul bows his knees to the Father so that three things can happen:

1. So that God can give to me and you empowerment in the inner man and engagement of the permanent indwelling of Jesus in my heart (Ephesians 3:16-17).

2. So that God can make me and you completely able to seize or grab what is the length, the height, the breadth and depth. (Paul does not complete the actual thought, but in v. 19 he tells us where he was going.) So that we can grab or seize the amazing love that is ours; and also that we can know the love that cannot be known. (Ephesians 3:18-19a NASB)

3. So that God can fill you and me with the complete fullness of Him. (Ephesians 3:19b).

This is what comes before the well-known Ephesians 3:20-21. It seems to me that we do well to focus on v. 14-19 to see what Paul has in mind before claiming v. 20-21. I would like to have us focus on v. 18 in particular.

In v. 19 we are told to focus on the love that Jesus has showered upon us. The word for "comprehend, seize or grab" used there is *katalambano*. It is a word that is full of action. In our passage, it is a middle voice infinitive. I point out the middle voice because I see it as an indirect middle which means I work at seizing or grabbing this amazing love for my own benefit.

Furthermore, the word indicates that I am to "attain definitively"[12] in the most positive sense. In reality this is what my life is about and in reality this is how I arrive at seeing Ephesians 3:20-21 occur more in my life.

So, how do we overcome this self absorption that is so easily among us? I was listening to Dallas Willard tapes a few years ago on leadership and spirituality. He was talking about how to engage leadership and growth. He described a concept he called the V.I.M.

V = vision
I = intentions/or passion
M = methods

He described it as a system that fuels itself. The reason why most Christians suffer or lose vitality in their spiritual life is their methods are not working effectively. Methods are Bible reading, prayer, worship, etc. Intentions or passions are the thing we are most excited about.

The man who loves to fish can get up at 2 a.m. to get to the lake or stream at the right time, but has trouble getting up for the 11 a.m. worship service. The vision is what drives it all. When my vision is biblical and healthy, that influences my passion and helps direct my passions to places the Father is pleased. My passions then fuel my methods in new ways, and those methods then continue to fuel the appropriate vision.

You can break into the cycle at differing places. The least effective place to break the cycle is at the method level. The better way to break into this is at the vision level or passion level with the goal of having more empowering methods. Once the empowered methods are set, then the other two pieces get their appropriate blood flow.

My wife is an oncology nurse and she often describes for me how the newer cancer drugs work. One particular set of drugs works at cutting off the blood flow to the tumor or cancerous cell. It literally makes the tumor die from lack of food; the drug starves the tumor to death! Often we have Satanic oncology drugs put into us to cut off blood flow to the key sections of our vision and passion. It's a terrible price to pay and something that must be avoided at all costs!

Significant Theological Commitment

As we plan for the harvest and beg God for more workers in and from the harvest, the production goal must be kept in mind. When we talk about people, what we wish to see is a great obedience to Jesus Christ and a tremendous theological robustness.

Because we are "planting churches," we cannot think that we can short cut on the theological integrity and commitment and training necessary to see new disciples made through this work in the harvest.

Skill

As we turn to the skill set side of ministry, we can focus on these seven skill-based matters that Dr. Charles Riddley has identified: (Dr. Riddley has identified 13 skills necessary for effective church planters, but I am only mentioning seven of them at this point.)

Ability to Visionize and Cast This Vision

Matthew 28:16-20: "But the eleven disciples proceeded to Galilee, to the mountain which Jesus had designated. When they saw Him, they worshiped Him; but some were doubtful. And Jesus came up and spoke to them, saying, 'All authority has been given to Me in heaven and on earth. Go therefore and make disciples of all the nations, baptizing them in the name of the Father and the Son and the Holy Spirit, teaching them to observe all that I commanded you; and lo, I am with you always, even to the end of the age (NASB).'"

Matthew 16:13-20: "Now when Jesus came into the district of Caesarea Philippi, He was asking His disciples, 'Who do people say that the Son of Man is?' And they said, 'Some say John the Baptist; and others, Elijah; but still others, Jeremiah, or one of the prophets.' He said to them, 'But who do you say that I am?' Simon Peter answered, 'You are the Christ, the Son of the living God.' And Jesus said to him, 'Blessed are you, Simon Barjona, because flesh and blood did not reveal this to you, but My Father who is in heaven. I also say to you that you are Peter, and upon this rock I will build My church; and the gates of Hades will not overpower it. I will give you the keys of the kingdom of heaven; and whatever you bind on earth shall have been bound in heaven, and whatever you loose on earth shall have been loosed in heaven.' Then He warned the disciples that they should tell no one that He was the Christ (NASB)."

2 Timothy 1:12-14: "For this reason I also suffer these things, but I am not ashamed; for I know whom I have believed and I am convinced that He is able to guard what I have entrusted to Him until that day. Retain the standard of sound words which you have heard from me, in the faith and love which are in Christ Jesus. Guard, through the Holy Spirit who dwells in us, the treasure which has been entrusted to you (NASB)."

2 Timothy 1:12-14 sums up this areas very well. Paul tells Timothy that one major thing has kept Paul going all this time. He mentions it two times—once in v. 12 and again in v. 14. Paul says that it was his conviction that the "treasure" (*paratheke*) he has guarded or entrusted to the Holy Spirit was safe until the day when it did not matter anymore, the day when he would see Jesus again at the rapture or death (1 Thess 4). In v. 14, Paul then directs Timothy to guard the treasure that has been entrusted to him by God.

The "treasure" (*paratheke*) that Timothy now has is a powerful thing. It was what kept Paul going. Anytime I can come close to figuring out what kept Paul going is a good day for me!

The "Treasure" (*paratheke*)

The "treasure" (*paratheke*) is used in Jewish literature about the most important of important—the thing that drives you at all times. Paul is saying that his treasure is Bema material and he is holding it for that day because it is there that he will have to give his accounting for what he has done because of his "treasure." So what is your treasure?[13] What is that to you?

I believe the treasure Paul is talking about is what we call the Great Commission, the most important mission point, the reason for all the reasons. Maurer says this word, in profane Greek or common Greek outside of religious references, says, "This object was to be kept free, unused and undamaged until restoration. The trustworthiness of the trustee was thus most important."[14]

Maurer continues, "Christ is able to protect and keep the Gospel committed to the community not only to the time of the first apostle who will soon depart, but through the storms of coming generations right up to the last day. The genuineness of continuity is established not by the transmitted teaching as such but by the One who is Himself its content."[15]

So, where does this leave us? The ability to visionize or centralize the gospel presentation to every aspect of church work and church planting is key to our task and is truly our treasure!

Ability to Self Motivate

1 Thessalonians 2:1-10: "For you yourselves know, brethren, that our coming to you was not in vain, but after we had already suffered and been mistreated in Philippi, as you know, we had the boldness in our God to speak to you the gospel of God amid much opposition. For our exhortation does not come from error or impurity or by way of deceit; but just as we have been approved by God to be entrusted with the gospel, so we speak, not as pleasing men, but God who examines our hearts. For we never came with flattering speech, as you know, nor with a pretext for greed—God is witness—nor did we seek glory from men, either from you or from others, even though as apostles of Christ we might have asserted our authority. But we proved to be gentle among you, as a nursing mother tenderly cares for her own children. Having so fond an affection for you, we were well-pleased to impart to you not only the gospel of God but also our own lives, because you had become very dear to us (NASB)."

Skill is needed to be able to self direct and self motivate. Church planting has a very diverse schedule and varied energy demands dictated by the clock. It seems Paul was quite able to impact people and what motivated him was the giving away of his life to others (1 Thess 2:8). Recognition of the need to have this skill developed and to allow God to form this in the planter is key.

Ability to Create Ownership in Ministry

Ephesians 4:11-16: "And He gave some as apostles, and some as prophets, and some as evangelists, and some as pastors and teachers, for the equipping of the saints for the work of service, to the building up of   the body of Christ; until we all attain to the unity of the faith, and of the knowledge of the Son of God, to a mature man, to the measure of the stature which belongs to the fullness of Christ. As a result, we are no

longer to be children, tossed here and there by waves and carried about by every wind of doctrine, by the trickery of men,
by craftiness in deceitful scheming; but speaking the truth
in love, we are to grow up in all aspects into Him who is the
head, even Christ, from whom the whole body, being fitted
and held together by what every joint supplies, according to
the proper working of each individual part, causes the growth
of the body for the building up of itself in love (NASB)."

The five-fold gift set mentioned here for Jesus to give to us to carry
out ministry is key. Paul, of course, being apostolic, pioneered new
churches wherever he went. Building or creating ownership in ministry is our key job. As addressed earlier, focusing in on the priesthood
of the believer is key.

Ability to Relate to the Unchurched

Acts 20:26-27: "And now, behold, I know that all of you,
among whom I went about preaching the kingdom, will no
longer see my face. Therefore, I testify to you this day that
I am innocent of the blood of all men. For I did not shrink
from declaring to you the whole purpose of God (NASB)."

This is powerful comment recorded for us by Luke about Paul! Oh,
that I could say that I am innocent from the blood of all men because
I declared the entire counsel of God to them!

This declaration of innocence reminds us of the watchmen of the
nation concept with which Ezekiel was charged by God. In Ezekiel
3:17-27 and 33 Ezekiel is told to tell the people what God has said. In
Ezekiel 2:1-3:11, we find how prepared Ezekiel was for his job. God
made his head as emery to be harder than flint (3:8) so he would endure this job. Ezekiel also was told to eat the scroll (2:8). Like John in
Revelation 10, so too, here, to eat the scroll and engage the bitter and
the sweet sensation God gives through this exercise is unique preparation for proclamation of the treasure that is ours to give.

Paul must have understood this concept uniquely to be able to
proclaim his innocence of all men. How I long for such a comfort!
May we achieve such a comfort!

1 Corinthians 9:19 and 23: "For though I am free from all men, I have made myself a slave to all, so that I may win more. . . I do all things for the sake of the gospel, so that I may become a fellow partaker of it (NASB)."

Paul shares his strategy of how to invest his life and allow people to become dear to him—to make himself a slave to people. Paul shares something very interesting in v. 19. Paul says he is free from all men, but he makes himself a slave to all (*pasin*). The dative use of "all" (*pasin*) indicates a perspective Paul has and shares. A use of the dative in advantage or interest indicates how Paul viewed himself. He was self motivated by sharing his life with others by seeing how he had made himself a slave to all people for their benefit through the gospel.

Spousal Engagement in the Planting Project

Ephesians 5:22-33: "Wives, be subject to your own husbands, as to the Lord. For the husband is the head of the wife, as Christ also is the head of the church, He Himself being the Savior of the body. But as the church is subject to Christ, so also the wives ought to be to their husbands in everything. Husbands, love your wives, just as Christ also loved the church and gave Himself up for her, so that He might sanctify her, having cleansed her by the washing of water with the word, that He might present to Himself the church in all her glory, having no spot or wrinkle or any such thing; but that she would be holy and blameless. So husbands ought also to love their own wives as their own bodies. He who loves his own wife loves himself; for no one ever hated his own flesh, but nourishes and cherishes it, just as Christ also does the church, because we are members of His body. *For this reason a man shall leave his father and mother and shall be joined to his wife, and the two shall become one flesh.* This mystery is great; but I am speaking with reference to Christ and the church. Nevertheless, each individual among you also is to love his own wife even as

169

himself, and the wife must see to it that she respects her husband (NASB)."

Healthy roles in the marriage relationship are absolutely key to seeing the "skill" side of the equation. It is hard to talk about marriage and skill in the same sentence, but necessary. There are a number of skill-based matters that need to be harvested in the marriage relationship. Paul focuses on the husbands loving and the wives submitting and respecting.

Ability to Build Relationships

Matthew 9:35-38: "Jesus was going through all the cities and villages, teaching in their synagogues and proclaiming the gospel of the kingdom, and healing every kind of disease and every kind of sickness. Seeing the people, He felt compassion for them, because they were distressed and dispirited like sheep without a shepherd. Then He said to His disciples, 'The harvest is plentiful, but the workers are few. Therefore beseech the Lord of the harvest to send out workers into His harvest (NASB).'"

Building relationships also comes back to motivation. Jesus' motivation is well expressed here in Matthew 9:35. He was working tirelessly to proclaim His own good news and healing people. His reason for doing all this beyond the missional nature of the endeavor was His complete compassion for people.

It was this compassion for people that led Him to beseech the Father for workers in His harvest. From this is the common thought that we must see workers in the harvest—but ones from the harvest. So we look commonly for those just from the harvest to work powerfully in the harvest.

Ability to Exercise Faith

Acts 16:5 (6-10): "So the churches were being strengthened in the faith, and were increasing in number daily. They passed through the Phrygian and Galatian region, having been forbidden by the Holy Spirit to speak the word in Asia; and after they came to Mysia, they were trying to go into Bithynia, and the Spirit of Jesus did not permit them; and passing by Mysia, they came down to Troas. A vision appeared to Paul in the night: a man of Macedonia was standing and appealing to him, and saying, 'Come over to Macedonia and help us.' When he had seen the vision, immediately we sought to go into Macedonia, concluding that God had called us to preach the gospel to them (NASB)."

As explained elsewhere, Acts 16:5 gives us a powerful expression of God's first regional, church-a-day movement. What I find fascinating under this topic of exercising faith are two things:

Paul must have been on the proverbial cloud nine! To work alongside God planting a church a day in the Asia Minor region must have been gratifying! But, what next? How do you top that? A friend of mine says, "May the Lord of the harvest give us two a day!"

Imagine being Paul and planting a church a day! But look now at his life in vs. 6-10. Luke tells us that he passed through Phrygia and Galatian regions not being permitted by the Holy Spirit to speak the Word of God there. What a different way of life!

He arrived in Mysia, trying to go in the region of Bithynia but the Spirit of Jesus said no! Back at Mysia they come to Troas and then, yes! Paul got the Macedonian call and knew where God wanted him to go and where he was allowed to go!

Imagine the faith necessary to keep going. How many "nos" can we take? How many can Paul take? We see how many he can "at least" take. Six geographical references, either regional references or cities. Six. God said no. Imagine the resilience Paul needed to continue after such a high of seeing God plant a church a day!

One of the key lessons Paul gives us is that when God says "no" it is acceptable. Just keep going. Find the next place that God does want. I may think Mysia is the place and have good reason to think it; but finding out what God wants is the powerful side of it all. The really revealing question is this: Do I have systems surrounding me that allow me to receive a "no" from God and continue on?

Many of my systems, if not all of them, are dependent on knowing what God wants and where a "yes" lives. But in reality there is much to learn in the "no." My "nos" are many and very instructive. I need to have a clear understanding of our current situation in the West.

Stetzer and Bird report:

> At present there are thirty-four western industrialized democracies in the world, including the United States. Unfortunately no church planting movements currently exist among the majority people in those countries. However there are such movements among western settings (Cuba), in industrialized societies (China), in democracies (many in Central and South America), and among majority peoples (many in Asia and Africa).[16]

Our understanding of success is important and key to managing and overcoming what inappropriate expectations can do to us. Church planting movements are defined as having rapid multiplication in starting new churches because they plant quickly and produce exponential growth.[17]

I need to have a clear understanding of what we need to engage to overcome our obstacles

I am using Stetzer and Bird's list:[18]

- **Fervent prayer:** What can I say? What will it take for us to figure out the need for prayer centers in churches; for robust individual prayer habits that seek God with all our strength in prayer?

- **Aggressive evangelism:** The simple side of this concept is to talk about Jesus as much as possible to people. Finding the opportunities and helping to create them is key.

- **Empower the laity:** As we allow God's army—the church—not the professional clergy, to march on, we will see this happen. If we do not allow God's army to march forward in this realm of church planting, we will not see it happen as we wish.

- **Intentional evangelism and church planting:** Aggressive evangelism is one aspect of the mindset necessary to see a great harvest. Intentional evangelism that results in church planting is the next phase.

- **Commitment to theological robustness:** A powerful commitment is necessary to see the robustly healthy disciple made. We all want it; we just need to do it.

Summary

From 1996 through 2002, there were only two mainstream books published on church planting. Between 2003 and 2005, there were 18.[19] The current literature, though not voluminous, does speak directly on church planting. This is a good thing. Though the field of church planting has diversified, I still see gaps in the church planting work. I see many very good models for church planting. May God use each of them in powerful displays of His work!

The more common models are expensive in their normal implementation. The GSE church planting process is not expensive initially. It can have financial cost as the pastor comes on the field and needs support. But the advantage this brings to the table is that the core group is formed and the direction or "fruit" of the plant is obvious to some levels of consideration.

The small church is normally spoken of negatively or in terms of failure. But we need to celebrate all forms of church, particularly the small church, since God has made so many of them. Moderate growth and highly efficient energy are key concepts to assist in celebrating small churches. All of this can come out of great vision expressed by non-professionals. May this day continue to be blessed as the non-professional rises to the top and plants churches.

Micropolitan church planting is necessary as we carry out the Great Commission. It is a great opportunity for biblical success. As we mold our expectations to move ahead, micropolitan church planting is most likely to produce smaller churches. They are most likely to be formed from smaller core groups and more difficult situations, in most cases because of smaller numbers of people to contact.

Postmodernism brings many tools of great benefit to the table of the church planter. We want to take full advantage of the culture in which Jesus Christ has placed us.

In all of this, we must all ask the question about expectations. What are my expectations in this endeavor? Do they fit or hit reality or a likely outcome that is consistent with everything else God is doing in similar situations?

The world is growing through multiplication. In the church, we are typically not doing any better than growth through addition.

Does that mean we need to get rid of all the current methods of church planting? No. We need to keep all we have, but be open to other models that have the best chance to release the incredible army of believers we have sitting passively in our churches.

The solution is best described as not getting rid of what we have, but using what we have while exploring more doors into the realm of the unsaved person. As we find more ways to access the world of the unsaved through church planting, we can energize more disciples to obedience.

Notes

[1]Schwarz, *The Strong Little Church*, 54; Bullard, *Pursuing the Full Kingdom Potential of Your Congregation*, 12-13.

[2]Quinn, *Deep Change*, 124.

[3]Stetzer and Bird, *Viral Churches*, 107.

[4]Ibid, 197.

[5]Brian McNichol, quoted in "Churches Die With Dignity," *Christianity Today*, January 14 1991, 69.

[6]Tom Clegg and Tim Bird, *Lost in America* (Loveland CA: Group Publishing, 2001), 30.

[7]Easum, "The Easum Report," March 2003.

[8]Hugh Halter, Classroom discussion, Zerorientation, February 27, 2007

[9]Nebel, *Big Dreams in Small Places,* 97-98

[10]Clegg and Bird, *Missing in America,* 138

[11]Stetzer and Bird, *Viral Churches*, 141

[12]Kittle, *Theological Dictionary of the New Testament*, 4:10

[13]Ibid, 8:162-164

[14]Ibid, 8:162

[15]Ibid, 8:164

[16]Stetzer and Bird, *Viral Churches*, 167

[17]Ibid, 168

[18]Ibid, 181-182

[19]Stetzer, *Church Planting Observations on the State of North American Mission Strategies*, 3

Chapter 10

PREPARING AND SEEING THE SOIL

"Anyone who doesn't take truth seriously in small matters
cannot be trusted in large ones either."
Albert Einstein

"Half this game is ninety percent mental."
Yogi Berra

"Streetwise people are smarter in this regard than
law-abiding citizens. They are on constant alert,
looking for angles, surviving by their wits.
I want you to be smart in the same way—but for what is right.
(Luke 16:8-10, *The Message*)

Most of our visions for reaching people for Jesus Christ are more self-centered than God-centered. At least mine are. It is more often than not, "all about me." I quickly realized through this journey that God is so wise to have not granted me what I dreamed for Him many years ago!

I enjoyed being able to listen to Rick Warren share devotions at Exponential 2011. The point of his devotional was simply this: if I am bored in ministry or if my ministry is not getting my full attention, it is because my vision is too small! He took us to Isaiah 49 where Isaiah and God talk, and God makes it very clear that He wants Isaiah to have a global vision of God's glory. If I have anything less or smaller, I will definitely compromise my ministry potential in some way.[1]

The issue is my own pride and working through that, fighting self rejection, and embracing acceptance before God through choosing of Jesus Christ for eternal life. This focus has deep implications. I truly want God to plant a new church a day in my region of Ohio. I truly do. God has done it before—and even in Ohio He has done it before.[2] But I have to work through all the reasons God is not doing this today.

As I contemplate that lack of church planting movemental thinking of Christianity in our continent, I think we all would benefit from the insight of others to guide our thinking and help us process what next steps might look like. Two men, Ed Stetzer and Bob Logan, have put good thought and research into this question.

Stetzer directs our thoughts to industrialization. What does industrialization have to do with church planting? It seems to have everything to do with it. Industrialization perhaps fuels my pride more than anything else.

Industrialization means that I am free to earn money and make a living any way I want. This hunger for money and eagerness to pursue anything I want is because of industrialization of our land. So, if this is true, how can I best see the soil?

One of the more freeing moments of life is growing older. The older I grow, the more (at least I think the more) I desire God's things. I desire to see with God's eyes, not my own. Preparing for the long haul is the best option for us in America. The longer it takes, the more it belongs to God. The more it happens quickly, the more it belongs to me and not God.

How long does it take to see something get "going" related to church planting? Bob Logan says seven to 10 years for movement development.[3] Ed Stetzer shares that a definition of a church planting movement is: a rapidly reproducing church movement of indigenous peoples—rooted in the culture in which they come.[4] He further shares that there are no church planting movements in America, not in any of the 34 industrialized nations of the world.[5] Zero.

The gospel penetrating the fabric of our culture is what is necessary for this to happen. This penetration of our culture is dependent on many things, including 1) Engaging the laity to carry on this work; and, 2) Building permission-giving systems when it comes to church planting.

Ed Stetzer shares that movemental Christianity has certain traits:[6]

Prayer. We all acknowledge the necessity of prayer. We all pass the quiz and even the test that nothing happens without prayer. But what Stetzer is talking about is prayer such as we (or I) have not seen in our time! Is that us? Unfortunately, most church planting is entrepreneurial planting, but not necessarily a "hugely" spiritual endeavor! We are describing a type of leadership when we need to be describing a type of prayer. What drives you to plant is what makes you burn out and crash! When churches begin to pray and sacrifice, then we are well on the way.

Intentionality of multiplication. This means that the way I win my first convert to Christ is how I win the 10,000th convert to Christ. In this thinking, everything should multiply, thus pervading the whole process and changing our landscape.

Sacrifice. We live in the day of economic downturn. Some churches are doing fine in the downturn; others are suffering badly. Sacrifice in a good economy and sacrifice in a bad economy must be two different things for us. If we wish to see movemental Christianity, we need to embrace and understand sacrifice—both financial and time investment. Salaries set on structures are gone in church planting movements; movements are among lay people, non-paid folks. We live in a post labor segmented society. Each phase of our culture is segmented up. What that means is I go to an M.D. for general health issues, an oncologist for cancer; a diesel mechanic for my diesel engine, and gas mechanic for my gas engine. Even the clergy is segmented in a social cultural setting. We have senior pastors, executive pastors, associate/assistant pastors, youth pastors, counseling pastors, church planters, bishops, etc. But most church planting movements are in non-labor segmented societies! The other side of this illustrates it as well. The church planter is the visiting pastor, the worship pastor, the Sunday School leader, teaching elder, executive pastor, and so on.

Reproducibility. Something is reproducible if it reproduces. Those things that are indigenous and tied to culture are more likely to reproduce. Small things reproduce more quickly; launching large is reproducible and is possible.

Theological integrity. All church planting movements have robust belief systems. These types of examples are ones in which it takes some level of passion to get involved.

Incarnational Ministry. We must be the ones who live and breathe what it means to incarnate ourselves in our ministry area. Incarnational ministry is the putting on of clothes of the area where I am now living and finding ways to eat and breathe all that is here. It is to find ways to bring the gospel to people in as many relevant ways as possible. This is the paradigm or system thinking. We all need it and we all use it. We use it in its most recognizable way when we try to bring about change!

Empowerment of God's people. We must have permission-giving structures. Credentialing systems is one place to begin the conversation. Balance is necessary. It is the living, breathing church of Jesus Christ, led and indwelt by the Holy Spirit that serves as the guard to our theology. As you contemplate the need to have guards at the door to protect our theology—and we must have this—it shows why differing systems are needed. Creating another credentialing system does not protect from heresy, but the church as a whole does. When the church functions, then protection from heresy is there. We can have permission-giving structures and also have protections from heresy. We would also benefit from a "system" that simply says "go plant."

Charitability in appreciating other models. This concept applies to the current state of the church. As we work at figuring out who we are and how we are to go about doing our mission, we need to have a very charitable attitude in these conversations and journeys. While we figure it all out, we must demonstrate a powerfully charitable way of interacting.

Scalability. Here we are talking about movemental Christianity, where scalable structures become resources to get us where we want to go. It is something that Christians can rapidly grow without hitting a wall or ceiling to stop that growth.

Holism. Holistic commitment to ministry—all of it for transformation

The problem we face in the West is, as Stetzer has referenced it, "the answer may not fully lie in what the church is or isn't doing, but rather what the church has become in the West."[7] Stetzer goes on to share how movements can happen:

Our western dilemma: The institutionalization of our life we can call ecclesionomics. Pentecostalism is the fastest-growing movement in the world and in church history. It has now become institutionalized and thus it is not growing as it once did. This process is natural and normal, but it is not good.

We also have ecclesionomics. There are certain economic factors that fuel other factors. How are the financial structures of the church helping or hurting the multiplication of new churches? We say it "costs" too much to plant, and this idea makes us look bad, thus we are not seeing the fruit of spending money for church planting; so we are not doing it. We are in the habit of building buildings to do church, and this keeps us from rapid church planting.

Our American Dilemma: Discipleship. We have dependent believers, not robust disciples. We need to see the fruit of robust disciple-making! Small communities with life-on-life action help build robust disciples

Our cultural dilemma is bifurcation; that is: "peasants" and "professionals." We are making clergification and co-dependence the norm of the day. We need to recover the priesthood of the indigenous believer. "Peasants" show us where these movements need to happen. We need "unskilled" labor leading the way, places where we all do something and have a few lords over us.

Western industrialized democracies is where clergification thrives. Since clergification thrives, co-dependence thrives. In this thinking, the church is driven by clergy not the church family; the work of God is not vested in His priesthood. The people of God are disempowered from the very power source we all want and need. We end up with a death spiral. This death spiral looks like this: In the famous

80 percent of the work is done by 20 percent of the people means the 80 percent who are not doing anything are the reproduced ones in our current systems.[8]

Bob Logan adds these thoughts:

1. Cultivate a clear and compelling vision.
   What do you really want?

2. Maintain a long-term focus.
   How committed are you to get there?
   What are you willing to give up?
   7-10 years of focus to get the direction.

3. Build guiding coalitions for change.
   Who is passionately committed to invest in this?

4. Focus on right things – link leadership development to core values.
   Where is the point of leverage?
   Where is pain? —entry with change
   Where is opportunity?

5. Provide powerful coaching.
   How can we best cooperate with what God is doing?

6. Gather to celebrate, reflect, and refocus.
   How can we further internationalize our efforts?
   Two days a month/three times a year with the right people

7. Invite others to join in the journey
   Who else? What next?[9]

Spiritual Soil Preparation
Diachronic Continuum

Movemental church planting has its roots in the Scriptures. Acts 16:5 describes a church-a-day movement after Paul's first and second missionary journeys. This gives me hope. We can look at what God has done to move us to a church a day in a regional movement. The specifics are encouraging!

Let us look at 1) Jesus' ministry and His influence on the region of Asia Minor; 2) God's work in the book of Acts that formed this church-a-day movement regionally; 3) Examine the time implications of this concept.

Jesus' Ministry Impacting Asia Minor: Preparing the Spiritual Soil

As I contemplate the flow of Jesus Christ's work in preparing the soil in Asia Minor, I see a clear effort to prepare the spiritual soil of the geographic region for church planting. Jesus' ministry had far reaching implications. The flow of His work is clear to us today as we sit as recipients to His work 2,000 years ago. The pattern of His work is helpfully clear after 2,000 years. We have the benefit of the Gospels and Acts. All of this information is helpful as we try to understand how much time is involved in evaluating regional movements.

Notice Jesus' own ministry. He fed 5,000 men in Matthew 14:13ff and subsequently fed 4,000 in Matthew 15:38. It is not hard to imagine such a large number of people coming from great distances, even from Asia Minor. That many people being introduced to Jesus' work is possible. These two events represent more than 20,000 people when we include women and children.

Acts 2:9-10

Acts 2:9-10 shows that people from Cappadocia, Pontus, Asia, Phrygia, and Pamphylia were present for the birth of the church. These were all regions of Asia Minor to which Acts 16:5 is a summary reference.[10] It is not unreasonable to presuppose a high likelihood that some of the 20,000 who were touched by the feeding of the 5,000 and 4,000 were people from Asia Minor. Indeed we have specific, detailed information of people from Asia Minor who were present when the church was born in Acts 2.

The reason for these people's journey to Jerusalem was for the feast of Pentecost. So, these people were Jewish or had Jewish proselyte lifestyles. Some of these same people may have already met Jesus in the previous three years. Either way, they are present when God births His church. Whether through personal interaction with Jesus or His disciples in the previous three years or the simply the birth of the church in Acts 2, these people have witnessed a powerful event that they eventually took home to Asia Minor.

God's Work in the Book of Acts

The book of Acts also helps us see the specific points God used to prepare for a church a day in a region. By following the threads of the narrative, we can see the following important events, which support my premise that God had previously prepared Asia Minor for a church multiplication movement as expressed in Acts 16:5. Some of the details in Acts 11:19 through Acts 16:5 are these:

Acts 11:19 shows the persecution that arrives to spread the gospel.

Acts 11:25-26 shows Barnabas and Saul working for one year, investing in and growing leaders, a clearly important thread for our consideration.

Acts 13:4ff shows that the gospel was in Cyprus, residing in a key leader named Sergius Paulus.

Acts 13:49 tells that the gospel spread through the whole region of central Asia (Pisidian Antioch).

Acts 14:11 shows the impact of an incarnational ministry. The message was understood; God in flesh had come to men!

Acts 14:27-28 demonstrates Gentiles receiving the gospel and Paul's extended stay in Antioch.

Acts 15:1ff tells of the Jerusalem Council meeting and returning a unified message, a clear demonstration of love in receiving each other even in division. These threads, pulled from among others, help demonstrate that Acts 16:5 is a narrative summary. I conclude the Holy Spirit was birthing at least a new church every day at this time in Asia Minor. Acts 16:5 focuses on a Jesus-based movement and thus a Jesus-based church (Cole 2005, 50).

This is a powerful story to consider. If these thoughts are accurate, God used 20-25 years to prepare the soil for His church multiplication movement. Dates accepted for Jesus' miracles in His public ministry are approximately AD 27-30, and an accepted date for the Jerusalem Council is about AD 50.[11] This timeline also shows that training, as reflected in these threads, is key.[12]

Implications of the Time Sequencing

In working with these ideas, we see that 20-plus years of work are given to us in the biblical narrative. As Jesus lifted His eyes to the harvest, He saw the time involved in that culture to see a church a day in Asia Minor (Acts 16:5). As we contemplate such thinking as a church-a-day movement in a region or state, or a two-hour radius or four-hour circumference of driving time, we come quickly to some disturbing thoughts.

What must I do to prepare for a 20-plus year movement development process or even a 10-year movement development process? Plus, there is no guarantee that there will be a movement at the end of this 10 or 20 years. Do I want to put my life into something that might not work out after all? I do need to point out that the 20-plus year marker is for regions with "nothing" going before it.

How Do I View the Soil in Such an Environment and Will It Really Take That Long to See Something Different?

According to Stetzer's comments, key thoughts for us to consider are:

How committed am I to these things?

1. Abundant, fervent prayer that builds bridges between the lost and God who is desperately seeking them. May this type of movement of the Holy Spirit stir us to passionate prayer for the harvest and church planting.

2. Abundant, aggressive evangelism. This is evangelism that is functioning at every level of life.

3. Empowered laity to be the people of God. The key to all of this is seeing the laity engaged in the movement so that those who are in the church do not need to get anyone's permission to go and plant a church or engage a movement of churches.

4. Intentional evangelism and church planting—not leaving either to chance but deliberately engaging every section or fabric of society for new churches.

185

5. Biblically coherent, theological robustness. A commitment to and accessible to every Christian—the foundation of God's theological power.[13]

From these ideals, it is powerful to see how long a movemental process can take. Many of us will be easily persuaded to think, "I can make this happen sooner." I would advise against any one of us thinking this. God, in His freedom, may choose to do something different, but the beauty of what He is doing relates to making sure who gets the credit, or better yet, the glory of such a movemental process. May God receive the glory of seeing souls saved by the gospel of Jesus Christ and His shed blood on the cross for us!

Movemental Christianity: How to Evaluate and How to Proceed

I believe in regional movements. That is, I believe that we achieve the greatest effectiveness when we focus on a regional implementation of missional, apostolic genius or DNA. I see Paul's work in his three missionary journeys as regional efforts. I see this as most helpful to what we are seeking because we can keep regular contact and fraternity available. When it comes to multiplying regional initiatives, what are some important components?

Recognize that we are all standing on someone else's shoulders

All regional movements, or any effectiveness missionally, comes because someone else has gone before us and done some kind of work to prepare the soil. This is important to recognize and embrace. As we are able to embrace such a concept, it will help us in evaluating where we are on the continuum of mission impact.

Define the region

In VisionOhio, we define a region as a geographic place accessible by a two-plus hour radius of driving or four-plus hour diameter of driving. In Ohio, this covers most of the state. All points are roughly two-plus hours away from the center of Ohio. This becomes important from the natural keys to movement ahead.

Beginning tools to use

In focusing in on a region and then considering what tools to use to be most effective, we suggest using vision, fraternity, and prayer.

Prayer: The most important piece is the one mentioned last. We presume prayer, but must never be found lacking in it. The kind of prayer we are talking about is prayer together with specific focus on the region. The importance of focused prayer by those willing to invest in the region is key. These folks are then able to take this prayer focus back to their respective churches and keep that prayer focus going.

Vision: Vision is the apostolic genius beginning point. Vision for a region is how we can best capture the passion to focus missional energy into a common region. This vision is one that is formed through the gathering piece which we address next. This become the key part of the glue to continue the focused energy.

Fraternity: Herein lies the rub. Fraternity. The willingness to call us out together to focus on a region. In our fellowship of churches, I began calling out or inviting pastors from our 60 plus churches to come together two times per year for a regional focus. This invitation began in 2003.

It is easy to be enamored by how wonderful it would be if everyone would come, if everyone would see the value of gathering together in fraternity to work together in a focused missional energy and vision. But…

Fraternity is the driving post that makes it all work. If we are not coming together in a region, then it will be more difficult to impact that region. But, please keep in mind a key concept that set me free as we walked this path in Ohio in our denomination—self- selection. I found it very important to allow those invited (I invited everyone) to self- select their own attendance. I am part of an autonomous-based church family. My church family shares only a Statement of Faith in common. What this means is we have a flat church governance system. It is in this context that self-selection is important. Each pastor is free to engage a regional or national effort or not.

It is common to work with the willing, to connect with those that hear the same drum beat. It can be very detrimental to the movement if some engage at a time not their time! I have witnessed time after time those whom I thought to be key people not present at a gathering, only to find out that God used the self-selection process to assist the movement, not hinder it.

As people are allowed to define by their own place with the Lord whether they should be a part of this regional movement, you are then free to make as much progress as possible as the Lord directs the hearts of His people. Others will become a part as time moves on and progress is made. But, it can be so very harmful if I "force" or "guilt" someone to come when they are not yet ready to engage such thinking or ready to be in this place of ministry at this time. Jesus is building His church.

Evaluation and Engagement

So how do I know how to begin something new in a region that does not have a missional effort? How can I evaluate where to begin?

I have found that crossing already existing systems or organizations within a denomination is needed. The basic idea is this: if the already existing system or organization were able to produce a church-planting movement or multiplication, it would have already. This may or may not be accurate, but I find it a safe beginning point. Most of our denominational systems within regions can do church addition. But if we desire multiplication then we seek some other "system" to see that happen.

We have district mission teams that coincide with our districts. For example, within Ohio in our fellowship of churches, we have four districts with three district mission teams. Our district mission teams have done, and are doing, great work. They have added churches to our fellowship. They do many things well. Some of them are collecting and dispersing funds, providing planter care, prayer support, and reporting center work. They also do an incredible job affirming church planting candidates. These are all critically needed efforts!

The formation of a regional system that crosses these sub-regional groups is something that I have found helpful. It allows us to build beyond what the sub - region is able to do. Our sub-regional teams are pastors who are already very busy doing effective ministry, and we are asking them to do more. We found that resources follow vision which follows relationship and does best in a regional context. This applies to human resources as well as financial resources.

Think beyond your already existing systems or mission teams in your defined region; or, if your region has one existing team, think beyond this particular team.

How do I best evaluate this? Since your new regional thinking will most likely not have the components necessary to sustain or move forward a regional movement or perhaps multiplication, recognizing whose shoulders you are standing on is helpful. Know who is currently in the region and is already thinking this way (movemental thinking). Perhaps the person has already graduated to heaven. Praise them and acknowledge their work to others for inspiration and affirmation. If they are near or around you, spend time with them.

Thinking beyond this existing team is important, but do not ignore them. Work hard at collectively identifying what they are good at and recognize that you do not need to recreate what you already have. In the same breath, recognize the pieces that are not present in this team you need to build.

From this, find out what is already present to help put together the necessary components. Tom Nebel does a good job describing what is necessary for a regional effort.[14] This is the type of thinking necessary and the type of system necessary.

Once this is done, work at building these systems with the pieces on the table. Find and include those who can help make this happen. Building team is key. It is commonly thought that personnel and money alone are what are necessary to plant churches. Not true. Vision and passion are much higher on the scale to movemental church planting than either of those.

Pulling the Trigger

Once the foundational work or survey work is done in exploring what God has already placed in that region, pull the trigger on a regional gathering emphasizing the three values: vision, fraternity and prayer.

Allowing self selection in this process allows you to meet those Jesus has prepared for such a time as this. Inviting all is a good denominational practice, but self selection is necessary. If you know your region well enough, you may need to do an invitation-only process to begin. This has advantage for traction because the issue to avoid is the well-meaning person who is there to intentionally drag their feet through the entire process. Since they feel they "belong," they feel it necessary to be there.

Mission and Synergy

As this process begins, the Lord will add His own synergy to the hearts of those that come and present themselves. A call to commitment is key in this process. You are well positioned to make this happen as you direct the time, giving extended times over to prayer for this missional work.

Seeing the Soil

Jesus has a lot to say about soil types. Matthew 13 and Mark 4 are two passages in particular. This process of regional engagement needs to be pursued with effective soil recognition or at least openness to the differing types of soil that exist.

Jesus tells us there are at least four types of soil:

The "beside the road soil"—Mark 4:15. These are instances where the seed of the gospel is sown and "immediately Satan" comes and removes it himself! I find it amazing that Satan himself removes this seed. He does not need to concern himself with removing the seed in other soils himself. He has other very effective tools already in place to kill their growth (affliction, persecution, worries, and deceitfulness of riches—an amazing array of tools). But Satan is most concerned about removing this seed from ever being able to grow. Perhaps Satan fears wind or rain would cause this seed to go some place else where it can grow!

The "rocky soil"—Mark 4:16-17. These are instances where affliction or persecution arise and they fall away.

The "thorny soil"—Mark 4:18-19. These are instances where worries of this world or deceitfulness of riches makes them fall away. The "good soil"—Mark 4:20. A good crop return in Palestine at this time was 7.5-fold, or a very good return was 10-fold. Jesus is talking 100, 60 or 30-fold. That would be of great interest to any farmer!

How we can develop good soil depends first upon recognizing what type of soil is in the region on which I am focusing. If I determine that I am working in rocky soil (because of the lack of growth or affliction or persecution), then I know the problem. Rocky soil in Jesus' day was not the inclusion of many rocks. Rocky soil in Jesus' day was a little bit of soil on top of a layer of bedrock. The rocky soil is a couple of inches deep and thus heat and the lack of moisture can kill the seed quickly.

The Hocking Hills part of southern Ohio has rocky soil. Sixty-foot trees grow in soil a few inches deep because the roots intertwine with everything else and this root system allows for the necessary nutrients to live. So it is for us spiritually. As I identify this type of soil, I allow that to form my strategy for a particular church plant.

Prayer and prayer walking remove a number of problems, but they require a lot of effort and energy.

Jesus also helps us by giving perhaps my favorite parable after the one listed above. I like the parable of the soils (or sower) because Jesus said I need to know it well (Mark 4:13). In Mark 4:26-29, we have the parable of the seed:

> "And He was saying, 'The kingdom of God is like a man who casts seed upon the soil; and he goes to bed at night and gets up by day, and the seed sprouts and grows —how, he himself does not know. The soil produces crops by itself; first the blade, then the head, then the mature grain in the head. But when the crop permits, he immediately puts in the sickle, because the harvest has come (NASB).'"

What I find amazing about this parable is:
The seed grows. How, I do not know!
I can go to bed and sleep.

Jesus told this parable in a way that made it very *vivid* to the listener.

The seed grows. Jesus promises us that the seed planted in soil will grow. It even grows in poor soil, and Satan fears the seed so much that he personally removes it from the soil! Either way, the seed grows.

I love any parable that tells me to go on with life. So often I have come to understand evangelistic practices that elicit in me a guilt-type response that, if I carry it to its consistent conclusion, I would not be able to sleep!

None of us believes in evangelism this way. None of us believes that I need not sleep to evangelize the world. Jesus is certainly showing us that "normal" life is important in the gospel or seed penetration and growth concept.

Jesus tells this parable vividly. In Greek there is a well-known mood called the subjunctive mood. The subjunctive mood has markers or words that go before a word to help us know when a subjunctive mood verb is being used. For the English reader, the word in Greek that is subjunctive is also spelled differently—and that helps a lot too. I can always identify one because of such things.

Ninety-nine percent of the time, when the subjunctive mood is used, these markers are present (*hina, hopos* etc). Here in Mark 4:26-29, Jesus not only uses the subjunctive mood without markers, but He does so five times! This means it would have been very vivid to the hearers. It might be likened to hearing a story or joke from one of your favorite story tellers or comedians. You just love the way they tell their story or jokes and it is very vivid to you! So, too, with Jesus here. To tell this parable with five "naked" subjunctives is electrifying and everyone there who was Greek-speaking would have been captivated! All those who heard this parable (without the markers that normally precede them) would have totally heard and leaned forward to hear more!

So, too, must I, as I am captivated by the amazing truth of this passage!

What I know is that the seed will grow when it is placed in the soil—any soil. But the better the soil, the better the growth.

One illustration of this point is from my own ministry. My wife and I spent almost 19 years pastoring a church on the southwest side of Columbus, Ohio. Something I found out in our first couple years there (early 1990s) was this. I asked a dear friend this question: "How many churches of 1,000 or more are there north of Route 70 in Columbus and how many over 1,000 are south of Route 70 in Columbus?" He thought for a moment and then said, "Churches over 1,000 in attendance north of Route 70, I would say over 100. Churches over 1,000 in attendance south of 70, I would say 12."

That hit me like a ton of bricks. The population differential between north and south Columbus was not a ten-to-one ratio, but the arbitrary markers I used did show a ten to one differential. What does that mean? For me it meant that in the previous generation, there were a number of faithful men and women who prayed and spread the seed in the area north of Route 70. South of Route 70 is the type of soil we have. So I worked hard at positioning our church family at doing soil preparation things. We focused on prayer matters and event-based things that let the community know we were safe.

I will not know until I get to heaven and Jesus tells me whether I saw that right or not. We did see seed cast and grow, but not as much as I anticipate Jesus will see in the time to come until we see Him!

There are times when we do fully engaging spiritual work, realizing we are more about cultivating than anything else. Ben Arment puts it well:

"You could easily interpret what I'm saying to mean that we should only plant churches in fertile communities, but nothing could be further from the truth. If you are called to be a cultivator, then by all means go. I was one of them. We need missionaries in the toughest parts of the world. For most of us, this is exactly the mission field where God leads us. And the Bible teaches that the greatest rewards will be given to those who face persecution and difficulty for the cause of Christ."[15]

Notes

[1]Rick Warren devotional time at Exponential Conference, April 28-29, 2011. My apologies to Rick Warren for any misrepresentation of his focus!

[2]Logan, Robert E. and Steven L. Ogne. Church Planter's Toolkit. Pasadena, CA: ChurchSmart Resources (churchsmart.com), 1995.

[3]Robert E. Logan, classroom notes, Ashland Theological Seminary, Ashland Ohio, May 14, 2009.

[4]Stetzer, "The Four Church-Planting Commissions," July 27, 2009

[5]Stetzer, "The Four Church-Planting Commissions," July 27, 2009

[6]Stetzer and Bird, *Viral Churches*, 169. The entire list here is Stetzer and Bird's.

[7]Stetzer and Bird, 2010, 170

[8]Stetzer, "The Four Church-Planting Commissions," July 27, 2009

[9]Robert E. Logan, classroom notes, Ashland Theological Seminary, Ashland Ohio, May 14, 2009. I again apologize to Bob for any misrepresenting of his ideas here!

[10]Longenecker, *John-Acts. The Expositors' Bible Commentary*, 246

[11]Kent, *Jerusalem to Rome: Studies in the Book of Acts*, 20 and 106

[12]Gupta and Lingenfelter, *Breaking Traditions to Accomplish Vision*, 23

[13]Stetzer and Bird, *Viral Churches*, 181 ff.

[14]Nebel, *Big Dreams in Small Places*, 105 ff.

[15]Arment, *Church in the Making*, 48

Conclusion
PULLING THINGS TOGETHER

What Jesus Christ is all about is an amazing story. He is about trans-
forming lives through His glorious gospel. He has chosen to have the
church penetrate our current culture and have us tell an amazing story about how He came to our earth for us. He willingly went to His
death on the cross and rose again on the third day. This resurrection
has empowered us in amazing ways to reproduce ourselves in others.

The church in Thessalonica was an amazing place. It seemed to
be a "regular" church. It was not as noble as the Berean church down
the road or as "carnal" as the Corinthian church further down the
road. What was amazing about them is what I believe to be amazing
about any church that is in existence today or yesteryear.

In 1 Thessalonians 1:1-10, Paul says this:

> "Paul and Silvanus and Timothy, To the church of the Thes-
> salonians in God the Father and the Lord Jesus Christ:
> Grace to you and peace. We give thanks to God always for
> all of you, making mention of you in our prayers; constantly
> bearing in mind your work of faith and labor of love and
> steadfastness of hope in our Lord Jesus Christ in the pres-
> ence of our God and Father, knowing, brethren beloved by
> God, His choice of you; for our gospel did not come to you
> in word only, but also in power and in the Holy Spirit and
> with full conviction; just as you know what kind of men
> we proved to be among you for your sake. You also became
> imitators of us and of the Lord, having received the word in
> much tribulation with the joy of the Holy Spirit, so that you

became an example to all the believers in Macedonia and in
Achaia. For the word of the Lord has sounded forth from
you, not only in Macedonia and Achaia, but also in every
place your faith toward God has gone forth, so that we have
no need to say anything. For they themselves report about
us what kind of a reception we had with you, and how you
turned to God from idols to serve a living and true God, and
to wait for His Son from heaven, whom He raised from the
dead, *that is* Jesus, who rescues us from the wrath to come
(NASB)."

What I find amazing is the DNA contained in this local church. Paul
indicates this local church was able to impact the entire region of
Macedonia and Achaia with the Word of God.

Please note that what Paul said was this:

"For the word of the Lord has sounded forth from you, not
only in Macedonia and Achaia, but also in every place your
faith toward God has gone forth, so that we have no need to
say anything (NASB)."

The word of the Lord sounded forth like a trumpet in the greater
area of Greece.

By way of illustration, the area contained geographically in Ohio
is approximately 40,000 square miles. Pennsylvania is 44,000 square
miles. When I Googled the square miles of Macedonia and Achaia,
hoping that borders are the approximately the same, the site gave me
a geographical region of approximately 42,000 square miles.

I was amazed and blown away! The geography that this local
church impacted is a region larger than the one I work in: Ohio! That
is amazing DNA!

I believe that same DNA that was in the Thessalonians' church is
in every living church today that preaches the gospel of Jesus Christ!

How can we re-imagine the church today, taking the already
existent DNA in us and mimicking the work of the Thessalonians,
who were not as noble as the Bereans?

I hope all the stories we can discover about new church plants
or existing churches impacting their own regions can be used to in-

spire us! I hope we can identify an area in which we can plant a new church using any method we can—even GSE!

I hope we can concentrate on robustly healthy disciple-making and efforts to pass on the insurance policy that Jesus used in His work. I hope that our understanding of the harvest can come as close as possible to that of Jesus' and our response to be that of Jesus', too.

May we re-imagine a way to take on an 8-20 year time slot to see if God would be so pleased to make a regional movement happen in our various areas for His sake!

May all this be pleasing to our Lord Jesus!

FUTURE THINGS
AND MOVING AHEAD

With this introduction into the GSE concepts, there are two levels of training available to help these ideas move ahead in your region. Each one has differing purposes:

GSE Training: Overview of Process

This training is designed for those who are more regional leaders or perhaps known as more apostolic in their regional leadership function. This training focuses on the bigger picture considerations when it comes to using the GSE process in church planting.

Specific focuses:

1. The values of using this GSE process.
2. Conceptual understanding of the gathering approach. In this section we look at specifics of the gatherer's job and function. We also engage proactive exercises to help us identify gatherers we have all around us.
3. Conceptual understanding of the shepherding approach. In this section we look at the specifics of the shepherd's job and function.
4. Further concepts to explore in implementing the GSE process. This section covers all that is left to begin implementing this model.

5. Our last section is a coaching time exploring what next steps look like based upon what the specific target area presents and how to move forward.

Goal: So that regional leaders in your own movement can train your own gatherers. This should be a considered a one-day training time.

Training for gatherers

This training is for both gatherer trainers (the group described above) as well as those who are specifically targeted as gatherers in the regional movement. This training is flexible as well; those who function in regional roles can benefit from the exposure to the process as well as specific gatherers exposed to the process.

Specific Focuses

1. An overview of the concept - the view from 10,000 feet down to ground level.

2. The use of "fishing pools" and missional connection applied to their gathering environment.

3. Exploration of biblical examples of gathering.

4. Various exercises to aid in the gathering process and help the gatherer understand this process and the vision of the new church plant.

Goal: So that gatherers and shepherds are trained for this important work. This should be considered a half-day training event, though it can be extended if helpful.

Regular coaching assistance is also available for further progress. Yes, there is information shared in the trainings that is not contained in this book.

For more information, please contact:
Dr. Tony Webb at *tony@gseplant.org*

BIBLIOGRAPHY

Arment, Ben. *Church in the Making*. Nashville: B&H Publishing Group, 2010.

Bauckham, Richard. *Bible and Mission: Christian Witness in a Postmodern World*. Grand Rapids: Baker Book House, 2003.

Berkhof, Hendrikus. *Christian Faith*. Grand Rapids: William B. Eerdmans Publishing Company, 1979.

Berkhof, L. *Systematic Theology*. Grand Rapids: Wm. B. Eerdmans Publishing Co., 1981.

Bevere, Allan. *Theology and Ministry in a Postmodern World*. Lecture, Ashland Theological Seminary, Ashland, Ohio, April 30, 2007.

Browing, David D. *Deliberate Simplicity*. Lincoln, NE: iUniverse, 2006.

Bullard, George W, Jr. *Pursuing the Full Kingdom Potential of Your Congregation*. St. Louis: Lake Hickory Resources, 2005.

Carson, D.A., Douglas Moo, and Leon Morris. *An introduction to the New Testament*. Grand Rapids: Zondervan Publishing House, 1992.

Carson, D.A. *Matthew*. In *Expositor's Bible Commentary*, ed., Frank E. Gaebelein and J. D. Douglas, 3-599. Grand Rapids: Zondervan Publishing House, 1984.

Clegg, Thomas T., and Bird, Warren. *Missing in America*. Loveland, CO: Group, 2007.

Cole, Neil. *Organic Church.* San Francisco: Jossey-Bass, 2005.

El Nasser, Haya. *For Political Trends, Think Micropolitan. USAToday,* 2004. http://usatoday.com/ (accessed 11/23/2004).

Bill Easum, "The Easum Report," March 2003, http://www.easum. com/church.htm

Fischer, Claude S. "Toward a Subcultural Theory of Urbanism." *American Journal of Sociology* (1975) 80:1319-41

French, Acts and the Roman Roads of Asia Minor p. 55 in David W J Gill and Conrad Gempf Volume 2 - *The Book of Acts in its Graeco-Roman Setting,* Grand Rapids: Eerdmans (1994)

Garrison, David. *Church Planting Movements: How God is Redeeming a Lost World.* Midlothian, VA: WIGTake Resources, 2004.

Gibbs, Eddie. *Church Next.* Downers Grove: InterVarsity Press, 2000.

Gladwell, Malcolm. *The Tipping Point: How Little Things Can Make a Big Difference.* New York: Little, Brown and Company, 2002.

Goodykoontz, Colin Brummitt. *Home Missions on The American Frontier.* New York: Octagon Books, 1971.

Gray, Stephen, and Short, Trent. *Planting Fast-Growing Churches.* St. Charles, IL: Church Smart Resources, 2007.

Gupta, Paul R., and Lingenfelter, Sherwood G. *Breaking Traditions to Accomplish Vision.* Winona Lake, IN: BMH Books, 2006.

Guthrie, Donald. *New Testament Theology.* Downer's Grove, IL: Inter-Varsity Press, 1981.

Halter, Hugh, and Smay, Matt. *And: The gathered and Scattered Church.* Grand Rapids: Zondervan, 2010.

Hirsch, Alan. *The Forgotten Ways.* Grand Rapids, MI: Brazos Press, 2006.

Hofecker, Terry. *Seminar on North American Church Planting.* Unpublished syllabus for directed study class for D.Min. at Ashland Theological Seminary, March 6-10, 2006.

Karkkainen, Veli-Matti. *An Introduction to Ecclesiology.* Downers Grove: IVP Academic, 2002.

Kinnamen, Gary D., and Ells, Afred H. *Leaders That Last: How Covenant Friendships Can Help Pastors Thrive.* Grand Rapids: Baker Books, 2003.

Kittel, Gerhard. *Theological Dictionary of the New Testament.* Grand Rapids: Wm B Eerdmans Publishing Company, 1987.

Kelly, Mark. "Study Examines Challenges Within Smaller Churches." Lifeway: *Biblical Solutions for Life.* http://www.lifeway.com/ (accessed November 25, 2008).

Kent, Homer. *Jerusalem to Rome: Studies in the Book of Acts.* Winona Lake, IN: BMH Books, 1972.

Logan, Robert E. Churches planting churches training tapes.

Logan, Robert E. Coach Training May 2009.

Logan, Robert E., and Ogne, Steven L. *Churches Planting Churches.* Alta Loma, CA: CRM New Church Development, 1995.

Longenecker, Richard N. *John-Acts. The Expositor's Bible Commentary.* Grand Rapids, MI: Zondervan Publishing House, 1981.

Malphurs, Aubrey. *Planting Growing Churches for the 21st Century.* Grand Rapids, MI: Baker Books, 2004.

Martin, Kevin E. *The Myth of the 200 Barrier.* Nashville: Abingdon Press, 2005.

McClendon, James Wm., Jr. *Doctrine: Systematic Theology, Volume II.* Nashville: Abingdon Press, 1994.

McIntosh, Gary L. *One Size Doesn't Fit All.* Grand Rapids: Fleming H. Revell, 1999.

Meeks, Wayne. *First Urban Christians.* New Haven: Yale University Press, 1983.

Metropolitan Statistical Areas, Micropolitan Statistical Areas, Combined Statistical Areas, New England City and Town Areas, and Combined New England City and Town Areas – 2003.

Montgomery, James. *DAWN 2000*. Pasadena, CA: William Carey Library, 1989.

Nebel, Thomas. *Big Dreams in Small Places: Church Planting in Smaller Communities*. St. Charles, IL: Church Smart Resources, 2002.

Newbigin, Lesslie. *The Gospel in a Pluralist Society*. Grand Rapids, MI: William B. Eerdmans Publishing Company, 1989.

Noll, Mark A. "Christian America" and "Christian Canada." In *The Cambridge History of Christianity: World Christianities c. 1815-c. 1914*, ed. Sheridan Gilley and Brian Stanley, 359-380. Cambridge: University Press, 2006.

Noll, Mark A. *A History of Christianity in the United States and Canada*. Grand Rapids, MI: William B. Eerdmans Publishing Company, 1992.

North American Mission Board. Defining the North American Urban Context, brochure, 12/2/2008.

Pastors of Excellence. Sandberg Leadership Center. Ashland Theological Seminary. Ashland, Ohio. PoE Journey in six retreats, 2006-2007.

Penner, Myron B. Editor. *Christianity and the Postmodern Turn*. Grand Rapids: Brazos Press, 2005.

Quinn, Robert. *Deep Change*. San Francisco: Jossey-Bass, 1996.

Regele, Mike; with Schulz, Mark. *Death of the Church*. Grand Rapids: Zondervan Publishing House, 1995.

Rowell, John. *Magnifying Your Vision for the Small Church*. Atlanta: Northside Community Church, 1999.

Ryrie, Charles Caldwell. *Basic Theology*. Wheaton, IL: SP Publications, 1986.

Saucy, Robert L. "The Presence of the Kingdom and the Life of the Church," *Bibliotheca Sacra*. 577:30-46, 1988.

Schaller, Lyle. *Looking in the Mirror*. Nashville: Abington, 1984.

Schwarz, Christian A. *The Strong Little Church*. Leadership 20:4:53-54, 1999.

Searcy, Nelson, and Thomas, Kerrick. *Launch: Starting a New Church from Scratch*. Ventura, CA: Regal Books, 2006.

Sjogren, Steve. *Community of Kindness: A Refreshing New Approach to Planting and Growing a Church*. Ventura, CA: Regal, 2003.

Smith, Glenn. Leadership Network. "Church Planting Overview: State of Church Planting USA, 2007." http://www.leadnet.org/papers (accessed November 4, 2008).

Smith, James K.A. *Who's Afraid of Postmodernism?* Grand Rapids: Baker Publishing Group, 2006.

Stark, Rodney. "Christianizing the Urban Empire: An Analysis Based on 22 Greco-Roman Cities," *Society of Religion* 52:1; 77-88, 1991.

Stark, Rodney. *Cities of God: The Real Story of How Christianity Became an Urban Movement and Conquered Rome*. San Francisco: Harper, 2006.

Steele, Steve. *A Case Study In Cooperative Evangelism: The Dawn Model For The Billy Graham Center Evangelism Roundtable "Toward Collaborative Evangelization"* October 4-5, 2002 *By Dr. Steve Steele, CEO Dawn Ministries* "Collaboration In The Dawn Strategy," 2002.

Stetzer, Ed, and Bird, Warren. *Viral Churches: Helping Church Planters Become Movement Makers*. San Francisco: Jossey-Bass, 2010.

Stetzer, Ed. "The Four Church-Planting Commissions," presented at the national conference of the Fellowship of Grace Brethren Churches, Columbus, Ohio, July 2009.

_____. *Planting Missional Churches*. Nashville: Broadman and Holman Publishers, 2006.

_____. "Church Planting Observations on the State of North American Mission Strategies. http://www.newchurches.com/tools--resources/research (accessed November 25, 2008)."

Thomas, Robert T, and Gundry, Stanley N. *Harmony of the Gospels.* Chicago: Moody Press, 1978.

U.S. Census Bureau. *About Metropolitan and Micropolitan Statistical Areas.* http://www.census.gov/ population/www/estimates/aboutmetro.html (accessed 1/25/2005).

Volf, Miroslav. *After Our Likeness: The Church as the Image of the Trinity.* Grand Rapids, MI: William B. Eerdmans Publishing Company, 1998.

Wagner, Peter. *Church Planting for a Greater Harvest.* Ventura, CA: Regal Books, 1990.

Wallace, Daniel B. *Greek grammar beyond the basics.* Grand Rapids: Zondervan Publishing House, 1996.

Warren, Rick. Devotions, Exponential Conference, April 2011.

Winter, Ralph. "The Two Structures of God's Redemptive Mission; contained in Foundations of the World Christian Movement," *Foundations of the World Christian Movements: A Larger Perspective,* Ralph Winter, Beth Snodderly, editors. Pasadena, Calif.: Institute of International Studies, 2008.

Wright, N. T. *Simply Christian: Why Christianity Makes Sense.* New York: HarperSanFrancisco, 2006.

VisionOhio. Staff Meetings, 2010.

ENDORSEMENTS

The Church needs theology and the church needs practical strategy. *Raising Rabbits, Not Elephants* is one of the most practical and strategic books on church planting to come across my desk in quite some time. I commend this book to church planters seeking a creative perspective on missional church planting.

Ed Stetzer
President, LifeWay Research,
Author, *Subversive Kingdom*

Practitioner Tony Webb gives us a great picture of how you can understand and implement the GSE approach to church planting. Both practical and engaging, this book unpacks how a gatherer, a shepherd, and an elder can team together to plant healthy, thriving churches.

Dr. Bob Logan
Church planter coach
Founder, Logan Leadership
Instructor, D.Min. program, Fuller Seminary

I know Tony Webb as a coach who coaches church planters. To be effective, a coach has to help break progress down into manageable steps. In this book, Tony has broken the process of church planting down into three easily accessible roles. That would've been a good accomplishment by itself, but then Dr. Webb goes even farther, showing you how to find each role and what to look for! And all through it, Dr. Webb meets you exactly where you are--ready with the occasional answer but more often, a really good question, just like an excellent coach would! Reading this book will challenge you in the best possible ways.

Jonathan Reitz
CEO, CoachNet Global

From a profound love for the church and a clear vision for expanding the kingdom, Dr. Webb has articulated an ancient approach to our obedient disciplemaking that is simple yet effective. This proven method of establishing new communities of faith has the potential to renew both established churches as well as whole movements seeking a fresh impact in their communities and beyond.

Bill Ludwig
Church Planter and Lead Catalyst for MissioChurch

I have followed Tony Webb's model from his doctoral research through first implementation and now into its use in church multiplication movements. I need to say only two things about it. First, it is biblical. Second, it works exactly as promised.

Dr. Terry Hofecker
Director, North American Church Multiplication Institute
Ashland Theological Seminary, Ashland Ohio